MANAGEMENT

MATTERS

The Practical Guide for New Managers or

Managers with Limited Training

DR. TIM PARKER

Preface

The book title *Management Matters* has a double meaning. First, it points out the fact that good management really matters to success. Nothing really happens without the effort of people, so the management and leadership of them are critical – "people management" matters greatly. Second, there are particular matters of management that every manager or leader needs to know. The field of management and leadership developed over the past 100 years to a point where it's difficult to focus on the important points that matter. This book addresses many of the topics that matter for managers.

The information in this book is for people new to managing or those who have been doing the job with little to no formal training. An article in the Harvard Business Review (https://hbr.org/2012/12/why-do-we-wait-so-long-to-trai/) pointed out the time difference, on average, between managers taking on the role and when formal training took place was about 10 years. I'm hoping this book gives new or untrained managers a place to start. The discipline of management is not easy or simple – it's complex and difficult because you have to deal with people (particularly their behavior) in an ever-changing work environment. As of the day I wrote this, Amazon listed 190,582 books for sale on leadership and 1,035,730 on management. That's a lot of advice. The good news is you don't need to know all there is on these topics, just enough to formulate and be confident in your own management framework. This book is meant to help you understand what management is and why it matters – to you, your organization, and your employees.

Table of Contents

Introduction

You just became a manager, or have performed the role for some time with no training. Congratulations on being selected to the management role – it's a big responsibility. So, what does that really mean? What is your role within the organization? And how do you go about performing that role?

The father of modern management, Peter Drucker, provides a wealth of advice on the subject. Most of what we think about management and organizations is based on Drucker's decades of experience and study.

In broad terms, the essential role of a manager is to make the resources under your control productive. That means selecting the right tasks to accomplish to meet your given objectives and do it efficiently. After all, without clear objectives that fit into the big scheme of the organization, how would you know if you are headed in the right direction? To paraphrase Drucker, management by objectives works when you know what they are - 90 percent of the time managers don't. If you don't know what your objectives are, find out. How can you select your tasks to perform and measure progress if you don't know what you are trying to achieve?

Another area of focus for a new manager is realizing how to be effective (as opposed to just being efficient). Effective managers efficiently perform those tasks that should be done. Some may be efficient, but on tasks that may not need to be done at all. Knowing the difference is being an effective manager.

Drucker separated the function of management (being a manager) into two parts - managing and leading. He used the term managing in the sense of knowing what tasks needed to be accomplished and measuring performance. We commonly use metrics to demonstrate these results - knowing what to measure and reaching goals is part of being a manager. Managing in this sense is more about measuring performance and results than actually performing the tasks.

The Art of Leadership: Leading, or performing the tasks through your staff is the harder part of being a manager since it involves the art of leadership. Your job as the leader (the term is meant as a function as opposed to a position in the organization) involves managing the attitudes and behaviors of the employees to enable them to be effective. Being successful at leading involves knowing the strengths of the employees (and focusing on those versus trying to fix the weaknesses) and possessing an understanding of human behavior. For example, a manager should realize each person responds to input differently and values things differently (in other words, one leadership approach doesn't necessarily work on everyone the same way). A good starting point in understanding leadership is a book by Daniel Goleman (and others) called "Primal Leadership". The authors address the critical component of emotional intelligence that many managers fail to understand.

A very effective book addressing what to stop doing as a manager is by Marshall Goldsmith – "What Got You Here, Won't Get You There". Goldsmith covers 22 behaviors of managers that they should stop doing since those behaviors really irritate everyone else (and greatly hinder performance).

As a new manager, realize most people seek a purpose in what they do (see Dan Pink's book called "Drive"). That purpose isn't just making a living to survive - it's typically to serve a higher purpose. To really be successful, find the higher purpose for your group. The idea is not to manipulate your employees to serve this purpose - it's to find the real reason you do what you do.

As you may now realize, being a manager may be more complicated than you first thought. It's a bit scary at first and takes practice. Managing is not a strength for everyone so if it's not a strength for you, it's not fair to you or others to stay in the role. Those who are good at it raise the performance of the overall organization and are appreciated for what they contribute.

The Business Framework – A Case for Leadership

Business in a fundamental sense is pretty straightforward. Ram Charan described the process in his book "What the CEO Wants You to Know" – you sell something (a product or service) for a bit more than it costs you to make a gain (profit), and the more often you sell it (velocity or turnover) the more you gain over time. And that's it – it's that simple. Sort of.

Of course, there are the issues concerning to whom to sell it and how to present it (marketing), and creating an edge for your product or service (strategy). Those are the mechanics of business. However, how business operates now is different than it was just a short time ago.

Business as we know it evolved from a much different beginning. Large business organizations began sometime near the turn of the last century according to Peter Drucker (who wrote multiple books on the topic). Before that period were farms and "mom and pop shops" or the like. Due to industrialization in the early 1900's, it made sense to create large manufacturing organizations to optimize profit. To make the large organizations work, the leadership structure resembled the only other large organizations in existence – the Army and the railroads. In these cases, the knowledge base was at the top of the organization (those who knew how the operations worked) leading to a command and control leadership model. This was also the period when Fredrick Taylor devised the scientific method of production, and the automobile and other manufacturing industries exploded in size.

In this framework, production and profit were the metrics of importance. Over the next several decades, technology grew to cause corporations to reassess how to operate. Peter Drucker developed multiple theories on how corporations should behave during this period of evolution. Eventually, many theories on corporate management were developed to include 'management by objectives' (a Drucker idea), theory X and theory Y (in the '60s), and others. A fundamental shift was where in the organization the knowledge resided. Whereas it used to be at the top of the organization, it now resides in the field – at the worker or 'knowledge worker' level.

The Impact: What does that mean to business leaders? You are no longer in control of production, at least not like you used to be. In many cases, those who work for you have business-critical knowledge that you do not have. Although you still have the responsibility for the business metrics, it's up to the knowledge workers who work for you to create the desired results. Those in leadership positions no longer have the ability to command production. They have to know how to influence the behavior of employees to achieve goals. They have to lead.

Drucker described "business" as a combination of management and leadership – management as the mechanics of production (processes, metrics, etc.) and leadership (influencing the behavior of employees to achieve goals). In the end, however, effective leadership drives excellent results. That means those in leadership positions who wish to achieve great results need to learn about Emotional Intelligence, effective leadership styles, and transformational/transactional leadership to name just a few key topics.

Nothing gets done without people taking action - so lead them well.

Why Leadership and Why Now?

The business world has changed significantly over the past several decades. If we look at the overall evolution of business, the need to focus on leadership is clear.

Here are some of the key milestones:

- In the late 1800s, there were very few large "business" enterprises or organizations - the railroads and the US Army were two of the largest.
- By the early 1900s, the manufacturing process was in full swing - Fredrick Taylor devised the scientific method approach making the process-driven business more efficient.
- WWI and WWII drove the emphasis on efficiency and large-scale organizations, generally focused on skilled labor.
- IBM, GE, and the automobile industry emerged with large organizations in the early part of the 1900s, generally employing the "command and control" model of management.
- Peter Drucker effectively wrote the first volume on modern management in 1954.
- The GI Bill sent many to college after WWII, resulting in a boom in MBA's in the 1960s and after (noting that the command and control model of management still ruled the day).

- Globalization of corporations happened in the latter part of the 1900s - they no longer were large national companies, but large international/global companies.
- The internet became a reality in the 1990s as did the proliferation of computers.
- Automation of manufacturing and the increase in education of the workforce shifted manufacturing overseas (where labor was cheap) and gave rise to today's "knowledge worker."

In short, business started out as farms and small shops. That evolved to a few large companies using command and control management. The workforce was generally separated into skilled labor and managers (although there were few middle managers at first). After companies grew into international corporations with the advent of computers and the internet, skilled labor was replaced by knowledge workers as the dominant labor source.

In a workforce dominated by skilled labor, the most knowledgeable "plumber" becomes the leader in the plumbing shop. It's a matter of efficiency since the skill can be learned by others relatively easily.

In a knowledge-based workforce, the leader of the shop may not necessarily know how to do the knowledge workers' job. The "boss" has to rely on the employees to know what they are doing to meet goals.

So, the management needed to evolve with the evolving workforce. Under the skilled labor model, command and control (and the fear of getting fired) may have worked since a replacement could be found rather quickly. With the knowledge worker model, the demand for capable workers is high. Command and control methods no longer work. Innovation and creativity are now in the minds of the knowledge workers. Command and control must give way to effective leadership, focusing on the effectiveness of the knowledge worker. And, effective leadership is a matter of behaving in a way that creates a positive work environment and maintains a positive attitude for the workforce.

For leaders, it is critical to understand leadership approaches, styles, and behaviors and when to employ them. The success of your company depends on it.

Are Managers The Real Target of Leadership Theory?

Jeffrey Pfeffer, Ph.D. outlined in his most recent book, *Leadership: BS*, a huge disconnect between the decades of leadership research and its application – namely, it doesn't work. He cites numerous examples where people in the C-suite continue to misapply (or just NOT apply) much of the theory outlined in the decades of research on leadership theory. Instead, he declares the better way to reach the top is the use, or misuse, of power and influence. What a shock to students of management and business!

Then again, maybe he nailed it. Maybe the real takeaway from his book is the leadership theory we all know and love really doesn't apply as much to the C-suite. Let me explain. Consider the idea of three levels of employees requiring three types of leadership for the sake of simplicity. You could view these levels based on a generalized motivational point of view:

- **Hourly Employee level** where motivation is to optimize pay per hour. Although loyalty is a huge factor, so is the pay rate. Finding the right balance is critical. The quality of the management is crucial to employee satisfaction. Hourly employees may sacrifice a level of pay to remain in a good work environment. To some degree, working for a meaningful purpose is a factor as well.

- **Middle Management level** where the pay rate is generally fixed and the hours worked can vary greatly. The balancing act at this level is between job satisfaction and engagement driven by fairness in pay and work/life balance. To a great degree, working for a meaningful purpose matters for retention.

- **Upper Management level** (also called the C-suite and defined by me as VP and above) where the compensation is determined by the persons to whom the VP reports. People in upper management can move further up the chain of command if they perform well over a long period of time. To continually do well, those at this level must have significant influence (power) and few competitors.

The Upper Management level differs significantly from the other two employee levels. In a sense, this level reflects more of a dog-eat-dog world. To avoid being replaced by an underling or someone who has ties with more senior managers, a manager at this level needs to make alliances with others at this level (particularly higher). They also limit the exposure of high performers within the group to limit possible competitors.

In my view, the motivations of the Hourly and Middle Management levels are similar to each other. They are concerned with the day to day success of operations driven by their individual efforts in general. What is important is making an income that is on par with others in a similar position, being developed for job progression, and finding meaning (purpose) in what they do.

In contrast, the Upper Management level is motivated by how well the organization performs, particularly on Wall

Street. Because of the competitiveness at this level, moving up (to company President or CEO) means doing all you can to look good and using all means at your disposal to do so. Politics and keen maneuvering are all important at this level.

Therefore, due to the motivational differences in the levels described above, the application of good leadership principles as outlined in the academic literature is not same. The "Leadership Industry" as described by Pfeffer really doesn't apply as much to the Upper Management level as it does to the other levels. In addition, the role model approach used often to describe super-CEOs (CEO-worship) may not be useful either – some the CEO stories may be embellished as noted by Jeffery Pfeffer in a separate article.

In the end, I think Jeffery Pfeffer was right to say the "Leadership Industry" has it wrong IF you consider the Upper Management level only. Leadership theory still applies to the rest of the workforce – although the Upper Management level should pay attention. That said, until their motivation changes, they won't.

The Two Required Functions of ALL Managers

Managers as a group generally accomplish a multitude of tasks. By definition, they manage something - an office staff, a group of people, a program or a project team. They oversee how to accomplish things and give direction to whoever needs it. Right? Is this what they are supposed to do?

Let's look at where managers came from to get a clue on what they are supposed to do. A century ago the business world was evolving from an agricultural economy into an industrial one. The position of manager didn't exist as a role in the early stages of this development. Sure, there were people in charge, but they were the engineers who essentially made the machines that produced the items the organization intended to make. The management structure, or "command structure", reflected to a great degree the management methods of the two predominant large organizations at the time – the Army and the railroads.

It wasn't until the 1940's that organizations developed into the industrial society – where companies like Ford, GM, and IBM grew to a size that required a managerial structure. During this period, Peter Drucker studied many of these organizations, becoming the "father of modern management". To that point, he viewed the evolution of the "manager" as one of the most significant achievements of the 20th century. He taught "management" before it was a topic of interest. He also produced 39 books on the subject and numerous articles on the topic over many decades – meaning he probably knew something about it.

The First Required Function: So, according to Drucker the fundamental function of a manager is to "make resources productive". That means effective (efficiently doing the right things) use of the materials and people under your charge. That requires metrics to determine if the right amount of material is used, the best equipment for the task is used, and the people are led well (have the appropriate amount of education and training, proper pay and benefits, and appropriate levels of motivation). Note that leadership is the more important aspect of making resources productive and a topic for another time.

The Second Required Function: Drucker stated the second fundamental function is to "cause no harm". I realize this is a broad statement that applies to a multiple of areas. The function really applies to a manager's view of the world and his or her impact on it. It means to cause no harm to the employer, the employees, or society in general. In other words, it means to do the right thing for all those involved in what you do. So, represent your company or organization as though it was your own; as a boss treat your employees with fairness and respect as if they were volunteers – because they are; and maintain a high ethical standard relative to all of your actions (no turning a blind eye to actions you know deep down are just not right – like dumping hazardous wastes, or asking those who work for you to accomplish work in an unsafe manner).

It really is that simple. The hard part is to learn what "management" tools are most effective (what you really need to measure), what leadership skills you need to learn, and where you draw that ethical line.

Managing Those with a Technical Background

The critical leadership skills required by IT project managers includes components of leadership concepts, leadership theories, and leadership styles (Kaminsky, 2012; Warner, 2012). Project success includes successfully managing the control of costs, the scope, the schedule, and growth of project requirements (Nixon, Harrington, & Parker, 2012). Project managers also require an understanding of how to employ emotional intelligence in a positive way. Emotional intelligence includes an awareness of self behavior and the impact of the behavior on team members. Managers who use their emotional intelligence maintain a positive and productive relationship with team members (Nwokah & Ahiauzu, 2010; Yusof, Kadir, & Mahfar, 2014). A key aspect associated with a positive and productive work environment relates to employee behaviors within the work environment. The work environment influences how employees interpret the actions of the project manager and organizational leaders (Avey, Reichard, Luthans, & Mhatre, 2011; Notgrass, Conner, & Bell, 2013; Xue, Bradley, & Liang, 2011).

Project managers require an understanding of these leadership skills and must learn to recognize the circumstances in which to employ these skills. Information technology project teams consist of several members integrating components of computer technology to achieve an organizational goal (Perez-Arostegui, Benitez-Amado, & Tamayo-Torres, 2012). Organizational leaders select the manager of an IT project based on the employee's technical knowledge as opposed to demonstrated project management ability (Karanja & Zaveri, 2012). Due to the technical nature of the information technology field, IT employees fail to gain adequate exposure to formal training in leadership or management. The lack of formal project management training inhibits IT employees as effective project managers (Karanja & Zaveri, 2012). Identification of the leadership skills critical to the success of IT project managers becomes paramount to enable an organization to remain competitive (Perez-Arostegui et al., 2012; Rivera-Ruiz & Ferrer-Moreno, 2015). The skills required by project managers include two major areas of focus consisting of managing the most tangible components of a project and leadership. Leadership refers to abilities in influencing stakeholders and establishing a positive work environment (Anantatmula, 2010; Nixon et al., 2012). The management components typically include measures of cost against the budget and tracking the project schedule to the desired completion date (Anantatmula, 2010; Nixon et al., 2012). Ineffective leadership by the project manager includes behaviors such as inappropriate use of power and poor communication (Anantatmula, 2010). In addition, ineffective leadership results from a lack of ability to relate well with others, socially referred to as social intelligence (Baumgarten, Süß, & Weis, 2015; Nixon et al., 2012; Rahim, 2014). A key leadership concept focuses on a leadership orientation model defined by tasks or relationships (Kaminsky, 2012). Managers using the task-oriented approach focus on identifying necessary tasks and tracking scheduled milestones. The task-oriented approach proves less successful as opposed to managing the relationships with project team members to increase productivity (Kaminsky, 2012). Prominent leadership concepts include the transactional-transformational model and the importance of emotional intelligence. Emotional intelligence refers to a leader's ability to recognize and control the impact of a leader's behavior on team members. Successful leaders alter self-behavior to improve team relationships (O'Boyle, Humphrey, Pollack, Hawver, & Story, 2011). Company executives may explore methods to minimize the negative impacts of ineffective project managers by identifying leadership factors used by project managers affecting project success. The leadership factors include the understanding of leadership styles, concepts, theories and considerations (DuBois, Koch, Hanlon, Nyatuga, & Kerr. 2015; Kaminsky, 2012).

Definition of Key Terms

The area of leadership employs several terms typically unfamiliar to the general population. The terms include types of intelligence considered important in describing attributes or characteristics of leaders. Other terms include behavioral characteristics of followers in response to the actions of leaders.

Emotional intelligence. Emotional intelligence refers to the skill a person possesses to monitor and control self-emotions, as well as sense the impact the person's behavior has on the emotions of others. Emotional intelligence is a leadership skill a person uses to adjust self-behavior in response to emotional reactions of others and oneself (Goleman, Boyatzis, & McKee, 2002).

Leadership. Leadership refers to the behavior of an individual related to influencing and motivating others to achieve goals. Leadership contrasts with the management activities of planning and controlling, such as measuring costs, schedule and quality compliance (Anantatmula, 2010).

Management. The term management refers to activities related to planning and controlling costs, schedules, and quality to satisfy stated goals (Anantatmula, 2010).

Organizational citizenship behavior. The term refers an employee's performance of discretionary, or voluntary tasks, which benefit the organization and exceed the tasks of a given job description. These behaviors positively influence the effectiveness of the organization and result from the attitudes of employees towards their supervisor, in general terms (Bambale, Shamsudin, & Subramaniam, 2011).

Organizational commitment. This term refers to the amount of loyalty and obligation an employee possesses towards the organization for which the employee works (Choong, Wong, & Lau, 2012).

Professional commitment. This term refers to the degree of loyalty and obligation an employee possesses towards the employee's chosen profession. A high degree of professional commitment may diminish the degree of commitment towards the employee's organization (Choong et al., 2012).

Project Manager (IT). The IT project manager term refers to the person appointed to oversee the team responsible for achieving specific goals and results related to one or more components of an information technology system. The responsibilities include managing traditional aspects of a project such as cost, schedule, and scope, as well as providing leadership for the team members (Ofori, 2013).

Project success. Project success includes multiple factors related to achieving cost, schedule, and quality of the intended goals, as well as satisfying the goals of stakeholders (Ika, Diallo, & Thuillier, 2010).

Social intelligence. This term refers to the skill of a person in relating well with others in social settings and the impact their behavior has on others. Social intelligence skill affects the relationship between the parties (Goleman et al., 2002).

Chapter 1: The Basics

Business and Management Components

The leadership topics selected for review were addressed in a handbook on leadership compiled by a leading academic researcher, Bernard Bass (2008), to gain a broader understanding of the field of study. Important topics include emotional intelligence, Theory X and Y, transformational leadership, servant leadership, participative leadership, situational leadership, belongingness theory, and authentic leadership. Authors of particular note include Daniel Goleman, Peter Drucker, and Robert Greenleaf.

Effective Leadership Concepts

According to Fulk, Bell, and Bodie (2011), Peter Drucker formalized the function of management based on his studies and worked with industries in the 1950's. Drucker published one of the first books documenting the practices of the profession of management. The book outlined the purpose of management from a functional point of view (Bildstein, Gueldenberg, & Tjitra, 2013; Fulk et al., 2011). The writings of Drucker indicate the purpose of an effective manager is to make the available resources productive (Fulk et al., 2011). The effective manager focuses on the two distinct areas that include management of activities, and leadership of people (Fulk et al., 2011; Bildstein et al., 2013). The managed activities include controlling funds and schedules. The leadership aspect focuses on influencing and motivating the people tasked to achieve the desired results (Fulk et al., 2011; Bildstein et al., 2013). Managers with effective leadership skills share a strong sense of clear goals and a sense of responsibility for those goals. Effective managers share a sense of responsibility with the team tasked to achieve the goals and a desire to earn the trust of the team (Bildstein et al., 2013). In broad terms, effective leadership includes the ability to entice people on the team in a positive fashion to achieve desired goals (Aydogdu & Asikgil, 2011; Babcock-Roberson & Strickland, 2010; Bildstein et al., 2013).

Prominent leadership theories. Theories on effective leadership comprise many forms and approaches in describing a framework for consideration (Boykins, Campbell, Moore, & Nayyar, 2013; Derue, Nahrgang, Wellman & Humphrey, 2011; Turner & Muller, 2005). Authors of theories describe leaders based on individual characteristics such as charisma, commanding style, openness, and empowerment behaviors (Turner & Muller, 2005). An approach by Killian (2012) included particular levels of intelligence of individuals, such as cognitive, social intelligence, or emotional intelligence. Nwokah and Ahiauzu (2010) related the degree of effectiveness to the individual skills in each of the areas. Other indicators include characteristics of personality types, such as Myers-Briggs Type Indicators. Also, the Big Five Factor model assesses attributes of personality suggesting a positive effect of characteristics such as openness and extraversion (Derue et al., 2011). The predominant theories relative to a stereotypical business setting emphasize the creation of a positive work environment through a focus on the emotional needs of the employees (Nwokah & Ahiauzu, 2010).

Team leaders employing servant leadership emphasize a focus on the needs of the team members as opposed to the activities of the group or goal attainment (Boone & Makhani, 2012; Choudhary, Akhtar, & Zaheer, 2013; Goh & Zhen-Jie, 2014; Harwiki, 2013; Hu & Liden, 2011; Parris & Peachey,

2013; Zehir, Akyuz, Eren, & Turhan, 2013). In other words, the leader in the context of servant leadership provides for needs of the employee primarily and then follows by leading the group (Goh & Zhen-Jie, 2014). The intent of the servant leadership approach focuses on the well-being of the employee with the overall goal of helping the organization (Boone & Makhani, 2012; Parris & Peachey, 2013).

The servant leadership approach incorporates several attributes focused on the interests of the followers (Boone & Makhani, 2012; Parris & Peachey, 2013). Servant leaders develop the employees by providing learning opportunities, offering growth assignments, and offering encouragement (Boone & Makhani, 2012; Hu & Liden, 2011; Parris & Peachey, 2013). Followers view servant leaders as authentic and accountable for their actions. Followers perceive servant leaders as willing to listen to others and willing to share positional power with the followers (Boone & Makhani, 2012; Choudhary et al., 2013; Goh & Zhen-Jie, 2014; Harwiki, 2013; Hu & Liden, 2011; Parris & Peachey, 2013).

Leaders using the servant leadership approach incorporate a contrasting viewpoint for achieving organizational goals versus many other approaches to leadership (Boone & Makhani, 2012; Choudhary et al., 2013; Goh & Zhen-Jie, 2014; Harwiki, 2013; Hu & Liden, 2011; Parris & Peachey, 2013). The servant leader subordinates self-needs and goals in favor of the needs of the followers (Hu & Liden, 2011). In comparison to the other employee-oriented leadership approaches such as the transformational leadership approach, the primary difference centers on the placement of leadership focus (Choudhary et al., 2013). The success of the servant leader depends on the mutual trust between the leader and the individual followers (Goh & Zhen-Jie, 2014; Harwiki, 2013). Trust in this sense includes the willingness of the leader and follower to rely on the other's expected actions while possessing little ability to control those actions (Goh & Zhen-Jie, 2014). Within the servant leadership framework, the leader and follower rely on each other to act in a predictable fashion (Goh & Zhen-Jie, 2014). The expected predictable action result from previous actions and the emotional relationship develops between the leader and follower (Goh & Zhen-Jie, 2014).

The success of servant leadership also depends on elements of organizational justice and integrity (Choudhary et al., 2013; Zehir et al., 2013). Followers and leaders in the servant leadership framework expect fair and ethical treatment in conducting the business of the team and organization (Choudhary et al., 2013; Zehir et al., 2013). Followers expect fairness in the processes related to making decisions and in the distribution of resources (Zehir et al., 2013). The resources in this context include pay, rewards, outcomes of disputes, and allocation of promotions (Zehir et al., 2013). Followers also expect equitable interpersonal treatment from the leader and other team members which include the means and quality of communication and supportive behaviors (Goh & Zhen-Jie, 2014; Zehir et al., 2013).

Team leaders and organizations benefit from the use of the servant leadership approach as a result of the mutual trust and relationships developed between the team leader and the team members (Boone & Makhani, 2012; Choudhary et al., 2013; Goh & Zhen-Jie, 2014; Harwiki, 2013; Hu & Liden, 2011; Parris & Peachey, 2013; Zehir et al., 2013). Under the servant leadership approach, team members increase the level of commitment to the organization resulting in higher levels of positive discretional behaviors (Hu & Liden, 2011). In addition, organizational performance, employee engagement, and organizational learning increase as compared to the traditional vertical leadership approach (Choudhary et al., 2013;

Goh & Zhen-Jie, 2014; Harwiki, 2013; Hu & Liden, 2011; Zehir et al., 2013).

One of the theories on leadership addresses the concept of the leader extending the leadership role to the followers or team members (Benoliel & Somech, 2014; de Vries, Pathak, & Paquin, 2011; Yan, 2011). Under the theory of participative leadership, the leader enables team members to engage actively in decision-making and problem-solving typically in a group forum (de Vries et al., 2014). Participative leadership occurs in formal and informal settings (Yan, 2011).

The performance of teams that employ participative leadership improved as compared to the performance of a traditional hierarchical or vertical leadership model (Benoliel & Somech, 2014; de Vries et al., 2011; Yan, 2011). Team members develop a level of trust with other team members and the formal leader due to the development of a sense of openness to discuss issues (Yan, 2011). Also, members of the team develop a tolerance to dissenting points of view creating a perceived safe environment for open discussion (Benoliel & Somech, 2014; Yan, 2011).

Leaders must recognize the circumstances in which participative leadership may be successful (Benoliel & Somech, 2014; de Vries et al., 2011). The leader's role includes moderating the discussion and collaboration among team members with the intent of maintaining a constructive environment (Yan, 2011). Part of the leader's role involves recognizing personality differences among the participants to determine which of them appear comfortable being open to sharing in the discussion (Benoliel & Somech, 2014; Yan, 2011). Some team members may appear safe or confident sharing information and resources with other team members whereas others may appear over-confident and create high levels of stress within the team (Benoliel & Somech, 2014). Additionally, the leader must recognize some team members may respond positively in the social setting and differently in the work environment (Benoliel & Somech, 2014). Team performance increases when the personalities and work environment of each team member are similar which indicates that leaders need to recognize differences in these attributes to optimize performance (Benoliel & Somech, 2014).

The shared leadership approach includes a distribution of leadership roles distributed among team members by the formal team leader (Bergman, Rentsch, Small, Davenport, & Bergman, 2012; Drescher, Korsgaard, Welpe, Picot, & Wigand, 2014; Huang, 2013; Park & Kwon, 2013; Stagnaro & Piotrowski, 2013; Wang, Waldman, & Zhang, 2013). Shared leadership is also referred to as distributed leadership, collaborative leadership, co-leadership, or emergent leadership (Park & Kwon, 2013). Additionally, the shared approach differs from the concepts of teamwork and cooperative behavior in that the team members arrive at the appropriate actions to take through the team member interaction (Wang et al., 2013). Teams employing this approach effectively become self-managing by enabling several team members to share influence within the team and with the formal team leader (Dresher et al., 2014; Stagnaro & Piotrowski, 2013). One key role of the formal leader includes recognizing the strengths of the team members to enable each team member to succeed in the area of strength (Dresher et al., 2014). The leader may also enable particular roles to evolve and shift among team members based on the needs of the team's schedule and other constraints (Dresher et al., 2014).

Sharing leadership roles with team members results in teams benefiting in a positive team performance (Huang, 2013; Park & Kwon, 2013; Wang et al., 2013). In particular, a single formal leader may not possess all the necessary capabilities required of a team. The capabilities include organizing tasks and priorities, maintaining supportive relationships within the team, providing strategic direction, and providing a realistic view of constraints (Bergman et al., 2012). The possible loss of the formal leader minimizes the impact on the success of the team by sharing the leadership roles (Bergman et al., 2012). The advantages to the individual team member of participating in the leadership roles include increased trust between team members and more accountability for the result. The team member also increases knowledge sharing among team members and increases cooperation and team cohesion (Bergman et al., 2012; Huang, 2013; Stagnaro & Piotrowski, 2013; Wang et al., 2013). The use of shared leadership provides a more accurate prediction of team effectiveness, and performance than traditional leadership by a formal leader (Park & Kwon, 2013; Wang et al., 2013). Teams that tend to benefit from using shared leadership include teams focused on knowledge-based work (Huang, 2013; Wang et al., 2013). Additionally, knowledge-based teams benefit from shared leadership when the team members share a peer to peer relationship with fellow team members (Park & Kwon, 2013).

Situational leadership theory relates to the behavior of the leader, the behavior of the followers and the particular situation (Bahreinian, Ahi, & Soltani, 2012; Burian, Burian, Maffei, & Pieffer, 2014; Mukherjee, 2012). Under the situational leadership theory, no one leadership model provides optimized productivity and employee satisfaction (Bahreinian et al., 2012; Burian, 2014). The approach selected by the leader depends on the capabilities of the leader, the capabilities of the followers, and the conditions of the particular situation (Bahreinian et al., 2012; Burian et al., 2014; Mukherjee, 2012). Additionally, the culture of the organization influences the selection of the leadership approach in regards to the approaches perceived as desirable for the work environment (Bahreinian et al., 2012).

In the framework of situational leadership, a leader considers the specific situation and the readiness of the followers to participate in four management principles (Bahreinian et al., 2012; Burian et al., 2014). The management principles include planning, or the use of resources to accomplish goals and organizing, or the establishment and use of systematic processes. The principles also include controlling or monitoring the compliance of followers in the use of policies and procedures. The other principle consists of leading, or the nature of the relationship between the leader and the followers that enable achievement of goals (Bahreinian et al., 2012). The leader assesses the conditions of a particular situation and the follower capabilities to determine the appropriateness of a leader-led or follower-led team (Bahreinian et al., 2012). The assessment by the leader focuses on the ability and willingness of the followers to accept part or the entire leadership role (Bahreinian et al., 2012). The leadership behavior from a situational leadership point of view depends on the assessed capabilities and willingness of the followers (Mukherjee, 2012).

In contrast, contingency leadership theory includes the consideration of leadership effectiveness as a function of the match between a leader's preferred leadership style and a particular situation (Mukherjee, 2012). Typically, organizational culture includes particular operating characteristics of the industry and the environment in which the organization operated (Prindle, 2012). The operating characteristics define the preferred leadership style on a continuum from task-oriented leadership to relationship-oriented leadership (Altmäe, Türk, & Toomet, 2013; Auer-Rizzi & Reber, 2013; Colón & Smith, 2012; Prindle, 2012).

In the context of contingency leadership, a leader employs a leadership capability suitable for the perceived situation (Altmäe et al., 2013; Auer-Rizzi & Reber, 2013).

Given a particular situation, the leader assesses the structure of the tasks necessary to accomplish goals and the relationship with followers. The leader also assesses the power of the formal position held by the leader relative to the followers. The assessment enables the leader to determine the appropriate leadership approach applying to the situation (Altmäe et al., 2013; Auer-Rizzi & Reber, 2013). The appropriate selection of leadership approach to the situation serves to mitigate the level of stress presented (Altmäe et al., 2013).

A critical aspect within the context of contingency leadership includes the ability of the leader to understand which type of situation matches the leadership approach of the leader (Altmäe et al., 2013; Auer-Rizzi & Reber, 2013; Colón & Smith, 2012; Prindle, 2012). Leaders who prefer task-oriented situations perform well in highly structured situations that require a leader with strong positional power (Altmäe et al., 2013; Auer-Rizzi & Reber, 2013). Leaders who prefer relationship oriented situations perform more effectively in situations with fewer structured tasks and do not require a leader with strong positional power (Altmäe et al., 2013; Auer-Rizzi & Reber, 2013). Individual leaders follow a preferred leadership approach that may not fit well in all situations (Auer-Rizzi & Reber, 2013). Due to the tendency of leaders to prefer a particular approach, it is easier to move a leader to a situation that matches the leader's preferred approach as opposed to attempting to change the leader's preferred approach (Auer-Rizzi & Reber, 2013). Additionally, the success of the leader depends on the match of leadership approach to the situation as well as the degree to which the followers enable the leader to exert influence (Auer-Rizzi & Reber, 2013).

Followers create a set of expectations of the leader considered most effective based on the follower's past experience as explained under the implicit leadership theory (Baser & Rofcanin, 2011; Powell & Butterfield, 2011; Salter, Harris, Woodhull, & McCormack, 2013). The attributes of a particular leader as perceived by a follower are compared to the attributes of the ideal leader as determined by the follower (Baser & Rofcanin, 2011; Powell & Butterfield, 2011; Salter et al., 2013). Followers base leadership perceptions on the leader's position within the organizational structure, philosophies, motives, personality, and experience (Powell & Butterfield, 2011; Salter et al., 2013). Other followers use perceived cognitive abilities for a comparison (Powell & Butterfield, 2011). The degree of compliance of the leader to the individual follower's expectations determines the level of acceptance and effectiveness of the leader. The compliance of the leader is particularity important in the circumstances when most of the followers possess a similar set of expectations (Powell & Butterfield, 2011; Salter et al., 2013).

The theories outlined in the section above indicate the complexity of leadership theory. Project managers require an understanding of the theories from an application point of view to achieve a level of effectiveness to succeed (Boykins et al., 2013; Derue, Nahrgang, Wellman & Humphrey, 2011; Turner & Muller, 2005). As outlined in the discussion on implicit theory, a project manager requires an understanding or sense of how project team members view leadership. By recognizing the leadership expectations or perceptions of the team members, the project manager may adapt to those expectations to achieve a degree of acceptance (Baser & Rofcanin, 2011; Powell & Butterfield, 2011; Salter et al., 2013).

A similar consideration for project managers focuses on the degree of leadership involvement by team members. Project managers possess options in the way the team members become involved in leading the team. As outlined in the discussion of participative and shared leadership, the project manager selects the appropriate level and method of delegated leadership tasks (Benoliel & Somech, 2014; Huang, 2013; Park & Kwon, 2013; Stagnaro & Piotrowski, 2013).

A significant activity for a project manager to accomplish includes an assessment of the environment in which the team operates. A project leader assesses team member capabilities to determine an appropriate approach to employ as discussed in the situational leadership section (Benoliel & Somech, 2014; de Vries et al., 2011; Yan, 2011). In a similar fashion, the project leader assesses the conditions to determine the appropriate match of the conditions to the leader's preferred approach (Altmäe et al., 2013; Auer-Rizzi & Reber, 2013; Colón & Smith, 2012; Prindle, 2012).

The project manager as a leader may elect to devote the leadership efforts to the needs of the team members. Leaders using this approach contributes minimal attention on other aspects of project management (Boone & Makhani, 2012; Choudhary et al., 2013; Goh & Zhen-Jie, 2014; Harwiki, 2013; Hu & Liden, 2011; Parris & Peachey, 2013). Team members gain a high degree of freedom of action under this servant leadership arrangement (Goh & Zhen-Jie, 2014). Project managers rely on a high degree of trust between the team members and the project manager using this approach (Choudhary et al., 2013; Zehir et al., 2013).

The effective use of emotional intelligence. Goleman et al. (2002) described the degree of emotional intelligence an individual possesses, as opposed to cognitive intelligence, as the critical attribute related to leadership effectiveness. Leaders require an understanding of human behavior to achieve a successful degree of effectiveness (Rivera-Ruiz & Ferrer-Moreno, 2015; Yusof et al., 2014). The effective leaders, therefore, require skills in recognizing how the leader reacts emotionally towards others and how others perceive the leader's reactions. Effective leaders also require skills in recognizing the emotional state of others, and how to control the leader's emotional response (Goleman et al., 2002; Nwokah & Ahiauzu, 2010). The leader's ability to recognize and manage the leader's emotions and understand other's emotions is critical to effective leadership (Nwokah & Ahiauzu, 2010; Yusof et al., 2014).

The leader's control of emotions includes the ability to achieve a sense of self-awareness and self-management (Goleman et al., 2002; Nwokah & Ahiauzu, 2010). The self-awareness component comprises recognizing the approach the leader uses and the impact of that approach. The component also includes realizing the leader's ability to react appropriately (Goleman et al., 2002; Nwokah & Ahiauzu, 2010). Self-management refers to the action taken by the leader in response to assessing the emotional situation (Goleman et al., 2002; Nwokah & Ahiauzu, 2010). Actions managed by the individual includes control of inappropriate emotional outbursts and maintaining a sense of optimism. The individual actions also include preparing for a change in approach should the situation dictate the change (Goleman et al., 2002; O'Boyle et al., 2011). The leader's ability to control emotional response establishes the leader's skill in personal management. Therefore, the leader requires significant skill in relationship management (Goleman et al., 2002; Nwokah & Ahiauzu, 2010; O'Boyle et al., 2011; Yusof et al., 2014).

The social recognition skills of the leader provide the leader the ability to respond appropriately from an emotional point of view (Goleman et al., 2002; O'Boyle et al., 2011; Yusof et al., 2014). To be effective in a response, the leader requires sensitivity to the situation and the emotional state of individuals. The leader also requires sensitivity to the culture of the organization (Goleman et al., 2002; O'Boyle et al., 2011). In addition, an effective emotional response by the leader includes sensitivity to the relationship with team members to maintain a positive working environment (Goleman et al., 2002; Yusof et al., 2014). The aspects of the relationship include maintaining a motivating vision, providing positive feedback and instilling a sense of teamwork (Goleman et al., 2002; O'Boyle et al., 2011). The leader's abilities in emotional assessment and the leader's response to that assessment comprise the second aspect of the leader's emotional intelligence (Goleman et al., 2002; O'Boyle et al., 2011; Yusof et al., 2014).

Project managers require a significant degree of emotional intelligence to create and maintain effective leadership (Goleman et al., 2002; Nwokah & Ahiauzu, 2010). Team members respond depending on how the project manager behaves and conveys information. In this regard, a successful project manager learns to identify the method and tone appropriate for the team. The assessment includes a sensitivity to the most effective language and presentation to converse with team members to achieve an expected outcome (Goleman et al., 2002; Nwokah & Ahiauzu, 2010). Also, the assessment incorporates an ability to recognize how the team members react emotionally to the leader. Project managers with high levels of emotional intelligence lead effectively.

A framework for leadership style selection. The leader's approach and activities in response to a situation constitute the leader's leadership style. The leadership style influences the emotional state of the individuals involved in the situation (Goleman et al., 2002; Muna, 2011). The differing applications of emotional intelligence create a framework of styles useful in describing leadership behavior. The framework includes the coaching style, pace setter style, visionary style, affiliative style, democratic style, and command style (Goleman et al., 2002; Muna, 2011). When used in the appropriate context or situation, the leader gains a positive result in the attitudes of team members (Goleman et al., 2002; Muna, 2011; Nwokah & Ahiauzu, 2010). The inappropriate use of a particular style by the leader results in the degradation in the attitude and emotional state of team members. The degradation results in ineffective leadership (Goleman et al., 2002; Muna, 2011; Nwokah & Ahiauzu, 2010).

Four of the leadership styles in the framework above result in positive effects on the work environment (Goleman et al., 2002; Muna, 2011). The leader who employs the visionary style presents employees with a very positive future state of the organization, which the employees may strive to achieve (Goleman et al., 2002; Muna, 2011). The leader using the visionary style provides employees the desired result with no direction as to how to achieve the intended end state. In this case, the means to achieve the end state remains at the discretion of the employees (Goleman et al., 2002; Muna, 2011).

The leader who employs the coaching leadership style enjoys similar positive results (Goleman et al., 2002; Muna, 2011). Leaders using the coaching style employ a mentoring attitude with employees by guiding the employees' development in many aspects of the job function. Leaders delegate much of the work to the employees to allow them to learn how to execute tasks (Goleman et al., 2002; Muna, 2011). Employees view the employment of the coaching style as too much oversight by the leader if the leader uses the coaching style poorly (Goleman et al., 2002; Muna, 2011).

The affiliative leadership style allows leaders who use it to create a positive environment through emotional connections (Goleman et al., 2002; Muna, 2011). A leader using the affiliative style employs extensive collaboration with the employees and focuses on the employees' emotional needs with the intent of keeping the employees happy (Goleman et al., 2002; Muna, 2011). Leaders who employ the affiliative style avoid conflict with employees displaying poor performance to keep a positive work environment, which other employees may resent (Goleman et al., 2002; Muna, 2011).

Leaders using the democratic leadership style create a positive work environment by encouraging employee participation in many aspects of the work (Goleman et al., 2002; Muna, 2011). Under the democratic style, leaders allow employees to voice positive and negative opinions on issues with the intent to achieve consensus on a course of action (Goleman et al., 2002; Muna, 2011). While leaders using the democratic style create a positive work environment, employees may feel frustrated by the lack of action and the extended consensus building process (Goleman et al., 2002; Muna, 2011).

The leader who employs the pace-setting style sets clear goals and expectations for the employees (Goleman et al., 2002; Muna, 2011). The pacesetting leader expects the employees to execute tasks on schedule with little room for failure and provides a minimal amount of guidance (Goleman et al., 2002; Muna, 2011). Although a leader using the pace-setting style achieves results in a short period, the high demands and expectations of the leader create tensions. The tensions lead to decreased performance over an extended period (Goleman et al., 2002; Muna, 2011). The leader using the pace-setting style employs few of the beneficial emotional intelligence attributes, which may lead to a negative work environment (Goleman et al., 2002; Muna, 2011).

A leader using the commanding leadership style finds success in urgent or emergency situations by the clarity in the directions given. The commanding style includes the expectation of full compliance by the employees (Goleman et al., 2002; Muna, 2011). The commanding leader allows no discussion of actions taken or questioning of decisions made (Goleman et al., 2002; Muna, 2011). Leaders using the commanding leadership style generate a positive work environment less often than when using other styles. Leaders using the commanding style minimize the use of emotional intelligence and portray a less caring attitude towards the employees (Goleman et al., 2002; Muna, 2011).

Another framework associated with styles of leading refers to a continuum based on how a particular leader views the motivations of employees (Burke, 2011; Russ, 2011; Sahin, 2012). Douglas McGregor developed the concept, referred to as Theory X and Y, considering the particular leader's view of employees. Leaders in this framework view employees as lazy and requiring extrinsic motivation to be productive at one extreme. Conversely, in the other extreme leaders view employees as intrinsically motivated requiring only general guidance and support (Burke, 2011; Russ, 2011; Sahin, 2012). The particular view of the leader leads to the selection of leadership style employed which results in a positive or negative relationship with the employee (Sahin, 2012). In addition, a leader may select a leadership approach anywhere on the X and Y continuum based on the leader's view of the particular employee. A leader may employ leadership styles associated with theory X for some employees, and styles associated with theory Y for other employees (Sahin, 2012). The view of the leader and the leader's relationship with each employee also determines the level of employee participation in decision-making (Russ, 2011). The leader's view of employees and the subsequent quality of the employee relationship significantly influences the attitudes and performance of employees (Burke, 2011; Russ, 2011; Sahin, 2012).

Project managers require knowledge of the range of leadership styles to create a successful team (Fulk et al., 2011;

Bildstein et al., 2013). Effective leaders realize the strengths and weaknesses of each style and understand the circumstances most appropriate for a particular style (Goleman et al., 2002; Muna, 2011; Nwokah & Ahiauzu, 2010). The circumstances include the specific working environment and the nature of the employees. An effective leader adapts the leadership style as the circumstances change (Aydogdu & Asikgil, 2011; Babcock-Roberson & Strickland, 2010; Bildstein et al., 2013). For example, a project manager may adopt the pacesetter style for a team working under a demanding schedule. In contrast, the same project manager may employ the coaching style for less demanding circumstances (Goleman et al., 2002; Muna, 2011). The selection of a particular leadership style depends on how the project manager views employees relative to motivational needs. A project manager who views employees as lazy may select a more directive leadership style such as the command or pacesetter style. Conversely, a project manager who views employees as self-motivated may elect to use a style that provides more team member freedom. The styles include the coaching or democratic style (Goleman et al., 2002; Muna, 2011). Leaders such as project managers require knowledge of leadership styles. Leaders also require an understanding of the appropriate situation in which to select the style that increases effectiveness and the chance of success (Goleman et al., 2002; Muna, 2011; Nwokah & Ahiauzu, 2010).

Contrasting leadership approaches. The framework of transformational and transactional leadership provides another contrast in leadership approach (Aydogdu & Asikgil, 2011; Liaw, Chi & Chuang, 2010). Leaders who use the transactional view expect performance by employees in exchange for rewards and withhold rewards for poor performance (Aydogdu & Asikgil, 2011). Transactional leadership creates an exchange or contractual type of relationship and provides a minimal inspirational incentive for employee performance (Aydogdu & Asikgil, 2011). In contrast, leaders using a charismatic or transformational leadership view achieve employee performance beyond minimal expectations (Liaw et al., 2010). Behaviors of transformational leaders include idealized influence, inspirational motivation, intellectual stimulation, and individualized consideration (Aydogdu & Asikgil, 2011; Liaw et al., 2010). The resulting benefits of transformational leadership include high levels of organizational commitment and a relationship based on trust as opposed to short-term rewards (Aydogdu & Asikgil, 2011; Liaw et al., 2010).

Some instances occur where the absence or minimal participation of project leaders produce a successful organization (France, Leahy, & Parsons, 2009; Lian & Tui, 2012). The circumstances include an atypical organizational structure with minimal layers of management, which enables project teams, including IT project teams, to freely collaborate and achieve goals (France et al., 2009). An important factor in the selection of leadership style or approach by the team leader focuses on the perceived competence of the team members (Lian & Tui, 2012). Team leaders who consider team members as possessing high levels of technical competence minimize the use of leadership styles requiring high levels of direction (France et al., 2009; Lian & Tui, 2012). The team leaders in these circumstances provide team members greater autonomy in achieving goals (France et al., 2009; Lian & Tui, 2012).

A project manager in the leadership role chooses the leadership approach perceived to optimize the success of the team. The selection of the approach depends on the project manager's view of the overall nature of the team (Aydogdu & Asikgil, 2011; Liaw, Chi & Chuang, 2010). Teams consisting of members who view extrinsic motivation as more important than other motivators respond to rewards for performance.

Team members who find the nature of the work more motivating than rewards require more emotional incentive from the project manager for performance (Aydogdu & Asikgil, 2011; Liaw et al., 2010). In the situation where the work itself provides the motivation for all team members, the project manager minimizes the leadership influence. The minimal level of influence enables the team to perform well (France et al., 2009; Lian & Tui, 2012). A project manager provides effective leadership by recognizing the type of motivators necessary for the team to perform effectively.

Considerations on team member behavior. People selected to be leaders of teams greatly influence the action, or lack of action, and behavior of team members (Avey, Reichard, Luthans, & Mhatre, 2011; Notgrass, Conner, & Bell, 2013; Xue, Bradley, & Liang, 2011). To create an effective team and achieve desired results, team leaders must realize how the team members may react to the team leader's behaviors (Avey et al., 2011; Notgrass et al., 2013; Xue et al., 2011). A team leader's influence may convey positive or negative impacts on the team members, creating beneficial or destructive behaviors by the team members (Notgrass, 2013). As an example, the team leader's behavior may affect how the team members take pride in the group, leading to a commitment to the task and attraction to the group (Notgrass, 2013). The leader's influence may enable open and dissenting views to be heard among team members and may avoid destructive conversations (Notgrass, 2013).

An important aspect of team leadership includes recognition of the types of factors that impact the performance of team members (Ayd, 2012; Thaliath & Thomas, 2012). The motivation-hygiene theory developed by Herzberg categorizes motivating factors as those which employees associate with the feeling about the particular job, or intrinsic motivators (Ayd,

2012; Thaliath & Thomas, 2012). Examples of intrinsic motivators include recognition of effort and achievement, the potential for growth, the level of responsibility, and the type of work (Ayd, 2012; Thaliath & Thomas, 2012). Intrinsic factors meeting the expectations of the employee may achieve high levels of job satisfaction leading to a positive attitude and higher performance (Ayd, 2012). Conversely, hygiene factors include extrinsic factors associated with aspects of employment such as the level of pay, company policy, and working conditions (Ayd, 2012; Thaliath & Thomas, 2012). Extrinsic factors do not necessarily generate job satisfaction for employees and reduce job dissatisfaction (Ayd, 2012). Leaders need to recognize how the intrinsic and extrinsic factors affect employee behaviors and the degree of influence the leader may have on each of the factors (Ayd, 2012; Thaliath & Thomas, 2012).

The team leaders set the climate in which the team operates by how the members of the team perceive the behaviors of the leader (Avey et al., 2011; Xue et al., 2011). Leaders who employ an empowering leadership approach create a knowledge sharing environment within the team (Xue et al., 2011). Knowledge sharing within the team significantly adds to the organizational performance by improving the social influence of each team member (Avey et al., 2011; Notgrass et al., 2013; Xue et al., 2011). An understanding of the influence of the social environment provides a team leader the ability to shape the team climate in a positive way (Xue et al., 2011). The positive aspects of the team climate that may be shaped by the leader's behavior include the level of trust between team members. Other positive aspects include the degree to which team members affiliate with the team, and the level of innovation by the team (Xue et al., 2011). A positive team climate derived by empowering leadership requires leaders who possess the skills to achieve these results (Xue et al., 2011).

Team leaders also impact the team members on an individual basis by affecting the psychological capital of each one (Avey et al., 2011). Team members display characteristics of positive psychological capital by demonstrating a sense of positive expectation for the future. Team members also show a sense of confidence, a strong desire to persevere, and a sense of resilience (Avey et al., 2011). The results of positive psychological capital include discretionary behaviors not associated with formal rewards such as extra efforts beyond normal expectations (Avey et al., 2011). Negative psychological capital results in counter-productive behaviors by team members in the form of resistance towards change and increased willingness to leave the team. Additionally, team members gain an increased willingness to violate organizational norms such as theft and to make unwarranted negative comments about team members (Avey et al., 2011). The team leader plays a critical role in understanding and establishing positive psychological capital. The positive capital leads to the positive team member behaviors that help to successfully achieve team goals (Avey et al., 2011; Notgrass et al., 2013; Xue et al., 2011).

A team leader consideration similar to psychological capital pertains to the expectations in the mind of the follower relative to the perceived commitments made by the employer (Epitropaki, 2013; McDermott, Conway, Rousseau, & Flood, 2013; Randmann, 2013). Followers create a psychological contract based on unspecified commitments made through observations of practices. Followers also interpret verbal commitments and assume promises based on association with the organization (Epitropaki, 2013; McDermott et al., 2013; Randmann, 2013). Communications with co-workers, other managers, and members of the human resources department contribute to the follower's interpretation of organizational obligations (Randmann, 2013). As a member of the organization, followers feel entitled to the perceived equal treatment received by other followers (Epitropaki, 2013).

Team leaders play a key role in setting the perceived expectations of followers due to the frequent interaction (Epitropaki, 2013; McDermott et al., 2013; Randmann, 2013). Followers view the team leaders as agents of the organization and possessing the ability to represent the organization in making commitments (McDermott et al., 2013; Randmann, 2013). As the employees' primary representative of the organization, team leaders represent the single-most influential factor in shaping the employees' psychological contract (Epitropaki, 2013; McDermott et al., 2013). Because of the strong influence team leaders possess, team leaders must maintain an awareness of how they may inadvertently convey an obligation (Epitropaki, 2013; McDermott et al., 2013; Randmann, 2013).

Another consideration for team leaders relative to the psychological disposition of team members includes the belongingness theory. The term belongingness refers to an employee's perception of value or need by the employee's co-workers, as well as a sense of fit within the work environment (Cockshaw et al., 2014). The sense of belonging and fit results from a fundamental human need linked to individual happiness (Sääksjärvi & Hellén, 2013). People desire to participate with others in sharing, helping, and achieving tasks and activities (Sääksjärvi & Hellén, 2013).

Team members perform assigned duties dependent on the perceived acceptance by individuals within an organization. The individuals include other team members or employees of the larger organization (Clark, Mercer, Zeigler-Hill, & Dufrene, 2012; Cockshaw, Shochet, & Obst, 2014; Sääksjärvi & Hellén, 2013; Sedgwick, Oosterbroek, & Ponomar, 2014). Team members view acceptance in terms of social support, the commitment of the leader and commitment of the group

(Clark et al., 2012). The sense of belonging by team members results from the perceptions created during interactions with the team leader and other team members (Sedgwick et al., 2014). Team leaders who fail to recognize the team members' need for belongingness risk isolating the team members and potentially cause the team member to withdraw from the team (Cockshaw et al., 2014).

One of the prominent concepts in the literature on leadership includes the idea of authentic leadership (Darvish & Rezaei, 2011; Dhiman, 2011; Erkutlu & Chafra, 2013; Gardiner, 2011; Mutlucan, 2011; Nichols & Erakovich, 2013; Peus, Wesche, Streicher, Braun, & Frey, 2012). Leaders employing authentic leadership perform duties in accordance with the leader's values and personal convictions in a consistent manner from the point of view of the followers (Darvish & Rezaei, 2011; Dhiman, 2011; Erkutlu & Chafra, 2013; Gardiner, 2011; Mutlucan, 2011; Nichols & Erakovich, 2013; Peus et al., 2012). The correlation between the authentic leaders' leadership behavior and the personal convictions and values result from an ethical viewpoint by the leaders (Nichols & Erakovich, 2013).

The concept of authentic leadership includes four components to describe the model (Darvish & Rezaei, 2011). Authentic leaders incorporate a high degree of self-awareness in the portrayed behaviors relative to their beliefs and values (Darvish & Rezaei, 2011; Peus et al., 2012). The self-reflection of the leaders provides clarity in the leaders' motives and feelings (Darvish & Rezaei, 2011; Peus et al., 2012).

The second component of authentic leaders includes the balanced processing of positive and negative views of leadership performance. Authentic leaders consider self-performance as well as the perceived view of the followers (Darvish & Rezaei, 2011; Dhiman, 2011; Peus et al., 2012). The alignment of values and beliefs constitutes the third component of authentic leadership (Darvish & Rezaei, 2011; Dhiman, 2011; Peus et al., 2012). The leader compares leadership behaviors and actions to the leader's motives. The leader also compares the degree of consistency in the leader's values and beliefs (Darvish & Rezaei, 2011; Dhiman, 2011; Peus et al., 2012). The fourth component consists of a review by the leader of the level of transparency relative to the relationship with the followers (Darvish & Rezaei, 2011; Dhiman, 2011; Peus et al., 2012). The four components serve as a mechanism for the leader to create and maintain a consistent and transparent leadership culture within the organization in which the leader serves (Darvish & Rezaei, 2011; Dhiman, 2011; Peus et al., 2012; Nichols & Erakovich, 2013).

Leaders exercise leadership duties on a continuum between authentic and inauthentic leadership (Nichols & Erakovich, 2013). A critical difference in authentic leaders and inauthentic leaders includes the ethics in exercising the leadership duties (Nichols & Erakovich, 2013). Inauthentic leaders succeed in motivating followers and achieving goals based on self-interests as opposed to basing performance on values and beliefs (Nichols & Erakovich, 2013). Inauthentic leaders appear authentic based on perceptions and sacrifice followers for the leader's self-interests (Nichols & Erakovich, 2013). While authentic leaders develop followers through mentoring and coaching, inauthentic leaders maintain a personal separation with followers, desire blind obedience, and practice favoritism (Nichols & Erakovich, 2013).

Trust between the leader and followers comprise a critical factor in the success of authentic leaders (Darvish & Rezaei, 2011; Dhiman, 2011; Erkutlu & Chafra, 2013; Mutlucan, 2011; Nichols & Erakovich, 2013; Peus et al., 2012). Authentic leaders maintain a high degree of trust with followers due to the perception of a match between the leader's words and actions (Darvish & Rezaei, 2011). The trust demonstrated by authentic leaders results in positive levels of psychological capital with followers (Erkutlu & Chafra, 2013).

Followers of authentic leaders demonstrate high levels of organizational citizen behaviors and job satisfaction (Darvish & Rezaei, 2011; Dhiman, 2011; Erkutlu & Chafra, 2013; Mutlucan, 2011; Nichols & Erakovich, 2013; Peus et al., 2012). Employees demonstrate a stronger sense of organizational commitment resulting in increased involvement and identification with the larger organization and the team with which the followers work (Darvish & Rezaei, 2011). The implied, or psychological contract components of the followers improve due to the clarity and consistency of the leader's words and actions (Darvish & Rezaei, 2011; Dhiman, 2011; Erkutlu & Chafra, 2013; Mutlucan, 2011; Nichols & Erakovich, 2013; Peus et al., 2012).

The concept of authentic leadership includes several difficulties in practicing the leadership approach (Gardiner, 2011). For example, some followers interpret ethical behavior and integrity differently than the leader (Gardiner, 2011). In other instances, leaders fail to possess clear communication skills leading to misunderstandings by followers (Gardiner, 2011). Also, some authentic leaders may exhibit an authoritarian approach inhibiting the open dialog with followers (Gardiner, 2011). Another area of difficulty focuses on the goal selection of the leader who may not conform to the understood goals of the followers (Gardiner, 2011). The position of authority held by the authentic leader influences the leader's behavior and enables the leader to control roles of each follower that may conflict with the follower's expected role (Gardiner, 2011). The difficulties limit the benefits of the authentic leadership approach (Gardiner, 2011).

Equity theory resembles the concept of the psychological contract in regards to followers feeling unfairly treated by team leaders or the organization in which the followers belong (Bell & Martin, 2012; Morand & Merriman, 2012; Skiba & Rosenberg, 2011; Tudor, 2011). An employee expects equitable or fair compensation for the contribution the employee provides (Bell & Martin, 2012; Morand & Merriman, 2012; Skiba & Rosenberg, 2011; Tudor, 2011). Employees compare output and compensation of others in the same or similar positions to their own (Bell & Martin, 2012). Employees perceiving significant discrepancies related to the comparisons modify their behavior by adjusting output to resolve the discrepancy. Alternatively, employees adjust their psychological position to justify or rationalize the discrepancy, or simply resign from the position (Bell & Martin, 2012; Tudor, 2011).

Employees may encounter other considerations impacting the job market before modifying their behavior due to perceived discrepancies (Skiba & Rosenberg, 2011). In the most recent economic downturn, companies gained significant leverage in negotiating compensation with employees (Skiba & Rosenberg, 2011). The job market shifted to more "at will" employment arrangements giving organizations the ability to allow employees to leave as each employee deemed appropriate without any compensation from the employer (Skiba & Rosenberg, 2011). In addition, companies shifted the ratio of their workforce to include more temporary and contracted workers. The restructuring enabled the company to restructure the labor force easily as warranted by economic conditions (Skiba & Rosenberg, 2011). The recent labor market trends limited the incentive and leverage of employees to resolve perceived discrepancies in the compensation for their output (Skiba & Rosenberg, 2011).

The team leader plays a key role in minimizing the negative impact of equity theory by recognizing changes in employee attitudes and behaviors (Bell & Martin, 2012;

Morand & Merriman, 2012; Skiba & Rosenberg, 2011; Tudor, 2011). Changes in pay rates provide a temporary increase in the employee's job satisfaction (Bell & Martin, 2012). The most significant contributions of the team leader involve demonstrating compassion, creating a positive and transparent work environment, and increasing socialization in the work environment (Bell & Martin, 2012; Tudor, 2011). Team leaders minimize the impact of the equity theory by allowing the employee to engage in job sharing. Leaders may also offer job rotations that provide a means for employees better to understand the roles of all the employees (Tutor, 2011).

A critical activity for the team leader includes creating a sense of trust and caring to defray the impact of poor employee attitudes. Poor employee attitudes result in high levels of employee stress, burnout, and turnover. The poor attitudes also create low levels of job satisfaction (Tutor, 2011). Increased levels of positive communication between the team leaders and employees improve employee attitudes and increase trust (Bell & Martin, 2012; Tudor, 2011). To further increase the levels of trust and improve employee perceptions, team leaders engage in high levels of participative decision-making. Team leaders also increase information sharing, collaborative goal setting, and offer positive feedback and rewards (Bell & Martin, 2012; Tudor, 2011).

Social exchange theory resembles equity theory with the follower or employee expectations focusing on social exchanges between the employee and employer (Cohen, Ben-Tura, & Vashdi, 2012; Hansen, Alge, Brown, Jackson, & Dunford, 2013; Wikhamn & Hall, 2012). The social exchange theory depends on the expected social behaviors between an employee and other members of the organization. The other members of the organization include organizational leaders and team members (Cohen et al., 2012; Hansen et al., 2013; Wikhamn & Hall, 2012). The employee perceives a level of organizational support from the organization based on experience and observed behaviors in the organization (Wikhamn & Hall, 2012). Based on the perceived organizational support, the employee develops a sense of obligation and belonging to the organization resulting in an emotional bond (Wikhamn & Hall, 2012). As a result of the bonding effect, the employee provides acceptable social behaviors in response to organizational social behaviors already provided. Additionally, employees favorably anticipate future organizational social behaviors (Hansen et al., 2013; Wikhamn & Hall, 2012).

A key result of the social exchange theory includes a positive and trusting relationship between the employee and the organization creating a set of normal work behaviors (Wikhamn & Hall, 2012). The benefits to the organization received from the employees include increased organizational commitment and positive discretionary behaviors (Cohen et al., 2012; Hansen et al., 2013; Wikhamn & Hall, 2012). The employee's perceived obligations resulting from social exchange expectations become a part of the employee's psychological contract (Wikhamn & Hall, 2012).

Team leaders play an important role in establishing the positive social relationships with team members (Hansen et al., 2013). Team members interpret the degree of ethical behavior by the organization and the immediate team leader as an indicator of the degree of positive social exchange commitment (Hansen et al., 2013). The degree of ethical behavior by organizational leaders moderates the degree of organizational commitment by the team member (Hansen et al., 2013; Wikhamn & Hall, 2012). The ethical behavior of team leaders provides a significant impact on employee commitment to the supervisor. The team leader's ethical behavior also provides a large moderating influence on the ethical behavior of other organizational leaders (Hansen et al.,

2013; Wikhamn & Hall, 2012). The recognition by team leaders of the impact of ethical behavior on team members' perceptions is important to the success of the project. How team members view these behaviors relative to social exchange theory become important to the success of the team (Hansen et al., 2013; Wikhamn & Hall, 2012).

The leader-member exchange theory refers to the quality of the relationship between the employee, or team member and the immediate supervisor, or team leader (Malangwasira, 2013; Zacher & Jimmieson, 2013; Zacher, Pearce, Rooney, & Mckenna, 2014). The nature of the leader-member relationship depends on attributes such as the level of trust, the level of respect, differences in attitudes and values. The relationship also depends on the interpretation of the role of the team leader and team member (Malangwasira, 2013). High levels of trust and respect between a team member and team leader result in higher levels of extra discretionary effort on the part of the team member (Malangwasira, 2013). In addition, team members gain higher levels of job understanding, job satisfaction and communications (Malangwasira, 2013). Team members exercise minimal or basic compliance to job requirements when the leader-member levels of trust and respect remain low (Malangwasira, 2013).

The degree of differences in the characteristics of the leaders and followers contribute to the success of a leader-member relationship (Malangwasira, 2013; Zacher & Jimmieson, 2013; Zacher et al., 2014). The nature of the differences relates to the amount of job experience, tenure in the position, gender, age and level of education (Malangwasira, 2013; Zacher & Jimmieson, 2013; Zacher et al., 2014). The level of communication between the leaders and members decreases as the degree of differences in the characteristics grow to create a less successful organization (Malangwasira, 2013; Zacher & Jimmieson, 2013).

Particular attributes of team leaders contribute to improvements in the leader-member relationship and the success of the team (Malangwasira, 2013; Zacher & Jimmieson, 2013; Zacher et al., 2014). Successful team leaders demonstrate compassion and empathy for team members, reflect on team and self-performance and display a high level of understanding of interactions between employees (Zacher et al., 2014). Team leaders who successfully recognize leader-member characteristic matches and possess critical attributes increase opportunities for team success. The team leader's successful recognition also provides a competitive advantage for the organization (Malangwasira, 2013; Zacher & Jimmieson, 2013; Zacher et al., 2014).

Project managers require an understanding of the influences on team members in the team environment to achieve effective leadership (Avey et al., 2011; Notgrass et al., 2013; Xue et al., 2011). The level of trust perceived by each team member is a significant factor in the overall behavior of the team member. The relationship between the project manager and the team member requires a significant level of trust. Team members rely on the project manager to provide consistent, honest and accurate information to maintain a positive attitude towards the work (Avey et al., 2011).

The team member relies on the organization to demonstrate a level of trust similar to the project manager. Each team member perceives a set of obligations and expectations from the organization based on formal and informal information (Epitropaki, 2013; McDermott, Conway, Rousseau, & Flood, 2013; Randmann, 2013). The obligations and expectations result from observed practices in the work environment and the actions of the project manager. Team members develop a negative attitude towards work when the perceptions and expectations become violated(Epitropaki,

2013). Project managers require a degree of sensitivity to avoid the violations of perceived obligations and expectations.

Project managers as leaders need to recognize how each team member associates with particular groups. The degree the team member establishes a positive association with the project team is important for the success of the team(Cockshaw et al., 2014). The project manager needs to realize each team member associates closely with other aspects of their lives (Sääksjärvi & Hellén, 2013). Project managers require a sensitivity of how the team members' affiliations interrelate to avoid conflict and enhance positive interaction.

Organizational Behavior of Technical Professionals

The behavior of technically oriented professionals such as IT project managers indicates several factors which may influence the IT project managers' attitudes and perceptions towards effective leadership concepts (Rivera-Ruiz & Ferrer-Moreno, 2015; Farr & Brazil, 2009; Galvin et al., 2014; Cho & Huang, 2012; Ramlall, 2012). Technical professionals, such as those within the information technology field, display markedly more commitment to the profession in which they work as opposed to a commitment to the organization (Cho & Huang, 2012). The level of employee commitment to an organization or profession refers to the employee's attitude towards, and psychological attachment to, the organization or profession (Choong et al., 2012). In an organizational setting, the lack of organizational commitment by the leader decreases the level of positive employee organizational citizenship behavior. Positive organizational citizenship behavior includes a willingness of the employee to provide extra work when not necessarily required to do so (Bambale et al., 2011; Choong et al., 2012).

Employees retain levels of commitment to organizations and their profession to some degree. Employees requiring specialized technical education to succeed, or an attraction to the specialized type of work, account for the greater loyalty to the type of work, or professional commitment (Choong et al., 2012). The high level of specialized education leaves relatively less exposure to the necessary teamwork and collaboration skills associated with effective leadership (Karanja & Zaveri, 2012). The result of placing an employee in a leadership position that focuses more on the technical aspects of the work environment lessens the effectiveness of the overall organization. The leader places less attention on the attitudes of other employees and more attention on the technical issues (Choong et al., 2012).

Murray (2011) indicated that followers of IT leaders prefer leaders with technological backgrounds and suggests the primary reason for poor leadership relates to a lack of skills in relating to people. Organizational leaders value the business skills of the IT leader more so than technical skills or leadership behavior (Badshah, 2012). Successful companies show a clear and positive difference in employing leaders with effective people skills, or social intelligence (Ramlall, 2012). A small number of technically oriented organizations possess a sub-culture of their own and do not necessarily require leaders with recognized leadership attributes (Murray, 2011).

Students in technical fields fail to gain the appropriate business education to support success in a leadership role (Farr & Brazil, 2009). Farr and Brazil (2009) pointed out academic deans of college engineering schools continue to base the curriculum on foundation documents over 50 years old that lack any support for non-technical classes. The education framework remains unchanged although authors of reports as current as 2005 recommended inclusion of leadership and business skills (Farr & Brazil, 2009). The academic leadership at engineering schools continues to produce technically competent and skilled engineers who lack the business skills to perform well in a leadership role. The engineers possess higher levels of professional commitment than organizational commitment (Farr & Brazil, 2009). For example, project managers for construction projects require team-building skills to complete technically complex projects successfully (Galvin et al., 2014; Ramlall, 2012). In many cases, the project managers lack the positive attributes needed for team leadership. The required attributes include social intelligence to meet all the completion goals (Galvin et al., 2014; Ramlall, 2012). In addition, they often possess negative leadership qualities that hinder the success of a team or organization (Galvin et al., 2014; Ramlall, 2012).

Employees in the information technology field fare no better in leadership preparation. Kaminsky (2012) indicated only 32 percent of IT projects succeed and identified the project leader as the critical factor in the success or failure. The role of a project leader requires an understanding of human behavior to achieve a successful collaborative team. However, organizational leaders typically select the project leader based on the project leader's ability to understand and use technical concepts. These concepts relate to cognitive intelligence, as opposed to the ability of the project leader to understand and communicate well with people, which relates to social intelligence (O'Boyle et al., 2011). The performance of these teams results from a basic transactional style of leadership or a reward system, as opposed to a higher performing transformational style (Xue et al., 2010).

The leadership of complex and technical work requires high degrees of collaboration and teamwork, and not the outdated command and control style of leading (Anantatmula, 2010; Karanja & Zaveri, 2012). In project management roles, technically oriented professionals excel at the technical aspects of projects and fall behind on promoting and representing the projects successfully to senior managers (Anantatmula, 2010; Karanja & Zaveri, 2012). Leaders of technically oriented projects perform well in an organizational culture focused on managing specific tasks. Technical leaders execute the management part of the lead role adequately. Few technically oriented leaders possess the necessary effective influencing skills to lead or positively motivate the team members well (Rivera Ruiz & Ferrer-Moreno, 2015).

Technical professionals such as IT professionals possess a stronger affiliation with the profession as opposed to the organization in which they practice the profession (Cho & Huang, 2012). The content of the formal education of IT professionals focuses on technical aspects of the profession. The educational content provides minimal exposure to skills related to social and other behaviors necessary for a leadership role (Farr & Brazil, 200; Galvin et al., 2014; Ramlall, 2012). The technical members of a project team focused on IT work may prefer a project leader with high technical skills (Murray, 2011). However, IT project managers lack the effective leadership skills necessary to provide successful performance consistently (Rivera-Ruiz & Ferrer-Moreno, 2015).

Summary

Management comprises two functional areas each of which contributes to differing views of success (Anantatmula, 2010; Nixon et al., 2012). Measurement of traditional activities of managing a project is one way to assess the success (Anantatmula, 2010; Nixon et al., 2012). These measurements include assessments on meeting budget goals, time requirement goals, performance goals, and scope goals (Anantatmula, 2010; Nixon et al., 2012). A separate and critical measurement consists of manager success measured in leadership effectiveness. Effective leadership includes the use of influence and motivation with stakeholders and team members to achieve goals (Anantatmula, 2010; Mishra, Dangayach, & Mittal, 2011). Managers with high levels of effective leadership skills succeed more frequently as compared to other managers (Mishra et al., 2011).

Managers require knowledge of the leadership factors of management to achieve success (Khaleefah, Rashid, Al Ajoe, & AL-Husien, 2014). The leadership factors encompass multiple theories on the application of leadership and an understanding of the important role of emotional intelligence (Karanja & Zaveri, 2012). Additionally, the success of the manager depends on the manager's understanding, correct selection and use of leadership styles (O'Boyle et al., 2011). The manager's ability to perceive considerations impacting the follower's behaviors influences the selection of the most effective leadership style (DuBois et al., 2015; Kaminsky, 2012).

Each theory on leadership includes a particular approach to leading a team. The participative theory and shared theory relate to the degree the leader involves the followers in the leadership roles (de Vries et al., 2014; Dresher et al., 2014; Stagnaro & Piotrowski, 2013). Under the servant leadership theory, the leader devotes the attention to the specific needs of the followers and minimizes other aspects of the leadership role (Boone & Makhani, 2012; Choudhary et al., 2013; Goh & Zhen-Jie, 2014; Harwiki, 2013; Hu & Liden, 2011; Parris & Peachey, 2013). Alternatively, leaders using the situational leadership theory evaluate the capabilities of the followers, the particular situation, and the leader's own capabilities (Bahreinian et al., 2012; Burian et al., 2014; Mukherjee, 2012). In a similar way, under the contingency leadership theory, the leader assesses the match between the specific situation and the leader's preferred leadership style

(Altmäe et al., 2013; Auer-Rizzi & Reber, 2013; Mukherjee, 2012). In all cases, the leader requires an understanding of the implicit leadership theory. The importance of the implicit leadership theory relates to the acceptance of the leader by the followers based on the followers' collective view of appropriate leadership (Baser & Rofcanin, 2011; Powell & Butterfield, 2011; Salter et al., 2013). The understanding of leadership theories by leaders provides a key component in succeeding as a project manager.

Performing successfully in a leadership role requires the leaders to relate well with other members of the organization. Leaders with a high degree of emotional intelligence achieve a more effective team (Rivera-Ruiz & Ferrer-Moreno, 2015; Yusof, Kadir, & Mahfar, 2014). The components of emotional intelligence include the ability of the leader to recognize how information is conveyed and how the recipients interpret the information. Effective leaders self-moderate the tone and content of information conveyed to maintain a beneficial relationship with others (Goleman et al., 2002; Nwokah & Ahiauzu, 2010). In a similar fashion, effective leaders maintain an awareness of how others react to conveyed information. Leaders employing emotional intelligence create more effective teams (Goleman et al., 2002; Nwokah & Ahiauzu, 2010; O'Boyle et al., 2011; Yusof et al., 2014).

A leader's selection of the leadership style to use influences the attitudes of followers. An aspect of the leader's decision on the leadership style relates to the leader's view of follower motivation as outlined in Theory X and Y (Burke, 2011; Russ, 2011; Sahin, 2012). Leaders who view follower as lazy may select a more directive leadership style. Leaders who view followers as driven by intrinsic motivations may rely on fewer directive styles. However, some circumstances may dictate a more directive style due to the nature of the work

(Goleman et al., 2002; Muna, 2011; Nwokah & Ahiauzu, 2010). The more directive styles include the pace setter and command style. The less directive styles include the visionary, affiliative, democratic, and coaching style (Goleman et al., 2002; Muna, 2011). An effective leader selects the most appropriate style for the circumstances.

Effective leaders consider other influences that contribute to the followers' attitudes and performance. An important consideration focuses on the nature of technical professions relative the commitment to the organization (Bambale et al., 2011; Choong et al., 2012). Technical professionals possess a higher commitment to the profession as opposed to the organization. The professional commitment influences the attitudes of the followers (Cho & Huang, 2012).

Other considerations for an effective leader include organizational factors impacting the followers. Effective leaders require an understanding of intrinsic and extrinsic motivators for followers (Ayd, 2012; Thaliath & Thomas, 2012). Considerations also include the relationship between the followers and the leader as well as the follower and the organization (Avey et al., 2011; Notgrass et al., 2013; Xue et al., 2011). The follower perception of similar compensation for conducting work similar to co-workers comprises another factor (Bell & Martin, 2012; Tudor, 2011). In addition, effective leaders maintain an awareness of perceived or implied contractual obligations by the followers (Epitropaki, 2013; McDermott et al., 2013; Randmann, 2013). Effective leaders maintain an awareness of the factors and considerations.

Organizational executives that increase the number of leaders with information technology backgrounds require an understanding of the impact on leadership capacity and overall organizational performance. Many frameworks exist to allow an organization to understand the desired and acceptable level of leadership attributes for individuals. The frameworks enable the organization to assess IT project managers in a position of leadership and assess candidates for leadership positions. Specifically, the organizational executives need clarity on how each IT project manager understands and relates to effective leadership practices.

Chapter 2: Additional Resources

Peter Drucker – The Discipline of Management

As noted earlier in the text, Peter Drucker essentially founded the discipline of management. During his decades of research, teaching, consulting and theory development he managed to write 39 books and numerous articles. Below I provided a few internet links to collections of his articles. I also listed several of his books in the reading list at the end of the book.

Drucker had a knack for predicting what would happen in the world particularly when it pertained to the business world. For example, he predicted the rise and severe impact of Hitler and the causes of his rise to power. He also coined the phrase "knowledge worker" and "knowledge economy" and the economic/business dynamics that surround those concepts. Although many see Peter Drucker as focused on business and economics, he referred to himself as being in the people business – what he saw as the ultimate key to economic/business success.

http://www.druckerinstitute.com/peter-druckers-life-and-legacy/
http://www.druckerinstitute.com/peter-druckers-life-and-legacy/a-drucker-sampler/
http://www.inc.com/articles/2009/11/drucker.html

Marshall Goldsmith – Organizational Behavior

Marshall Goldsmith, Ph.D. is a world-renowned consultant focused on organizational behavior. Goldsmith and

Drucker collaborated on many projects and shared similar philosophies on behavior. He generally provides coaching services to corporations and high-level organizational leaders, although much of his work is applicable to most managers, at least for concepts to consider.

I listed few of his books in the reading list all of which are worth reading. He also shares his concepts online through his web page and on YouTube (which are particularly interesting to review). Below are some links to Goldsmith's work:

http://www.marshallgoldsmithlibrary.com/html/marshall/resources.html

https://www.bestpracticeinstitute.org/blogs/itemlist/user/5390-marshall.html

http://www.inc.com/author/marshall-goldsmith

http://thinkers50.com/sharing/marshall-goldsmith-video-blog/

Daniel Goleman – Emotional Intelligence

Daniel Goleman raised interest and focus on the idea of emotional intelligence (EQ) as being a critical component of leadership and a significant factor in organizational success. Social intelligence is also associated with (EQ) and performance of managers. Goleman was not the first to address EQ as a business concept but did conduct significant research on it and made it a major topic of discussion on organizational leadership. In the reading list, I noted one of the key books by Goleman (and others) on the topic.

Additional Topics on Management

The remainder of this chapter includes topics of particular interest to managers. Management is a complex topic that can't be covered in its entirety in one book (although Bernard Bass tried to create one using 1516 pages – "The Bass Handbook on Leadership", see the reference list).

7 Keys to Great Leadership…or is it 5, or Maybe 257?

We all have read articles that describe important attributes, or activities, or capabilities of great leaders. It seems one pops up daily on one social network or the other, or on all of them. They also seem to never end. Each providing sound advice that usually is of value.

Should those interested in leadership take each article as gospel? Is leadership really a matter of remembering all the keys in each article? In my view – yes and no. Here's why –

Leadership is a complicated matter. I know this based on a research paper I'm writing on the topic that requires me to research the history of leadership from the caveman days until now (not really since I'm not sure the cavemen documented any of their lessons learned, but you get the picture). That research covered a lot of ground to include The Bass Handbook of Leadership, a 1516 page book that weighs 5.2 pounds. Although I'm inspired to list all the books and papers I've read on the subject, let's just agree that there are a lot of views on leadership (one of the reasons leadership is not easy).

One of the principals I gathered on leadership involves three components – the leader, the followers, and the environment in which they operate. Changing one of these components may require changes in the other two. For example, a chief of a fire brigade may take the "command and control" approach during an emergency situation as he or she should. In this instance, there is little time or room for discussing the preferred approach to fighting a fire – the environment demands a very structured approach to leading and following. Once the situation is over and the brigade is back in the firehouse, the leadership approach may be softer and the followers more able to offer suggestions.

The entire idea of leadership is to inspire others (followers) to achieve desired organizational goals. The leader may or may not be the person in the formal leadership position – he or she may be an influential person within the group. My point is leadership depends on influencing the behavior of others within a given environment, which in many cases is dynamic and ever-changing. So, can you as a leader depend on just 7 keys to leadership, or 5? And if so, which 7 or 5 are best suited to your followers and/or your environment?

Don't get me wrong, I'm not saying these articles have no value – each article covers important topics. My point is to realize the context in which you work and see how the article applies. In your circumstance 7 key points may hit the mark, or maybe tomorrow's article will cover the 5 key attributes you really need. Or maybe you really need to carry the Bass Handbook around for a while (I hope not). In any case, keep your eyes and mind open since leadership is not a simple talent that can be boiled down to just a few key things.

Are You Really Listening to ME?

A previous new boss, the VP of my group, and I just began a conversation in his office with the door closed to keep it private. I sat across his desk not more than three feet away. It took us several days to find time to connect...and then the phone rang...and he picked it up.

The questions that ran through my mind were these:

- Was the caller more important than me who was actually present in the room?

- Does the boss think I or my programs are not important or worth the time we set aside?

- Does the boss treat everyone this way, by essentially giving them a signal he really isn't interested?

I ran across an article that covered communication skills. It began talking about the communication skills of Bill Clinton, which are extraordinary and part of his success. The opening few paragraphs described how he makes the person with whom he is speaking feel as if they are the only person in the room. He gives them his full attention making them feel important. Regardless of your political leanings, you have to admit that is an extraordinary skill.

Further in the article, it outlined another habit we all see that conveys the message they are not really listening, or that what we have to say is not important. Here it is, word for word:

"While our digital habits have rewired our brains for shorter attention spans, it's possible to reverse the process", says Tumlin. "Commit to minimizing or unplugging electronic distractions, and seek out meaningful in-person interactions".

"I'm not a guy who thinks all new technology is bad, but real connection doesn't happen through a device," says Tumlin. "Be willing to temporarily set aside screens and give your full attention to the person in front of you."

As you meet with others one on one, or in a meeting think about the hidden messages you are sending. Do the others feel they are important and really worth your time and attention? Will they feel like you really were listening once the meeting is over?

How to Assess Your Organization in Only 5 Questions

A group of recent graduates asked my advice on creating a new and exciting startup company. The initial discussion included a flurry of ideas and excitement about the company's potential. Each of the three partners brought complimentary talents, strengths, and value to the enterprise. The question for me was: Where do we begin?

I turned to Peter Drucker, the management expert for guidance.

The initial question for the group focused on Drucker's fundamental question – The purpose of the organization is to create….what? On this the group offered several replies - profit came up first, with money a close second, then growth. According to Drucker, the appropriate reply is "a customer". Without the focus on customers, the organization would fail.

Now that we had a focus, we began with the questions:

What is our mission? In other terms, what is the purpose of the organization – what are we trying to do? This is where the leadership gives meaning to the organization so others have a personal connection to the work.

Who is our customer? Said differently, who are you trying to serve with your product or service? Although it sounds easy, there are primary customers and secondary ones. The primary ones may be the end-users, and the secondary ones are those who have an interest in the overall outcome of the product or service. By answering this question, you can also determine who your customer is not.

What does the customer value? Or, what attributes of your product are customers looking for that may help them? Again, the product value may be different for the primary customer and secondary customer. One of the best ways to determine this is to ask the customers (not all of them of course, but enough to give you a sense of what is important).

What are our results? Are you meeting the needs of the customers? Are you providing the value they desire? Again, getting feedback by asking them is a good way to determine your success.

What is our plan? What are the next steps to achieve your goals? Or should you adjust your current approach considering the answers to the first four questions? What actions must be taken to develop new goals? What products should be abandoned? What risks should be assessed, etc. (based on Drucker's book – "The Five Most Important Questions You Will Ever Ask About Your Organization")

Needless to say, we didn't get through all of the questions in great depth. The partners left with plenty to think about. Each of the five questions incorporates supporting questions and other considerations making them easier to understand and more comprehensive. In addition, the questions apply to every type of organization – for-profit and non-profit alike. Drucker's intent was to provide a framework for organizational leaders to create an effective organization.

In the case of this startup company, the excitement is just beginning.

The Purpose of a Business is to Create …(?)

Money, or profit? Certainly required to stay in business. No doubt the finance-driven MBAs would agree to this answer. That said, if one was not worried about risk, then robbing banks would be the best approach to reach this goal.

Jobs? Maybe, and certainly from a labor and economic point of view. But, just having employees and filling jobs does not mean a successful business.

Let me give you a hint by telling you about my recent trip to New Hampshire to move my son into his new home. The effort involved driving from North Carolina in a convoy of four vehicles with many back roads to avoid tolls (nice scenery but it lengthened the trip significantly). During the stops for fuel, I noticed similarities for each location in which we stopped – all were less clean than we hoped for and the staff not as helpful as they could be.

That trend got me thinking about what was going on. Each operation was identical in that the staff was not well trained and the facility poorly kept – almost untouched from a maintenance point of view, or so it seemed. Not once did I think to myself "I should here visit again and soon".

Ultimately, I realized they were after a particular type of customer – the ones that don't necessarily come back. These customers would be "drive-by" ones that just fill up on gas and drive on to a distant destination. There is no intent to attract them to come back since these customers live in far away places. Therefore, the restrooms and surrounding areas are less than spotless (I'm being kind here) and the staff is not interested in being overly helpful (being kind again). Although I'm generalizing, we've all experienced these sorts of places on the road. Although not all are like this, many are and on purpose to minimize costs.

So, back to the original question. According to Peter Drucker (the revered management guru) the purpose of a business is to create...(wait for it, wait for it)....a customer. To do so, the business needs to ask what does the target customer value? In the case outlined above, it's a quick stop for gas (assuming no expectation of a return visit). And that's what the customer gets – a gas stop and little else.

Looking at a gas station that has the expectation of repeat customers (like the one up the street from where you live) I suspect the dynamic is different. The staff might be friendlier and make an attempt to connect with frequent clients. The restrooms might be cleaned, or at least checked a few times per day. The food and drink items may seem more palatable based on the overall appearance of the facility. Clearly, the target customer, in this case, has different expectations and values than the customer discussed above.

The lesson to be learned for any organization is to determine who your target customer is and what they value. The second part of this arrangement is to measure the results – are you actually providing the expected value to your customers? One of the best ways to find this out is to simply ask them – get feedback by talking to them (not all of them, but enough to get a sense of what's missing or what is hitting the mark). I discovered a great example of customer focus in New Hampshire where the McDonald's and Panera restaurants offer – get this – lobster rolls with real lobster obtained locally. That's customer focus.

In summary, the purpose of an organization (business or non-profit) is to create customers. You have to know and offer what they value, and measure your results. If you are off the mark, you need to develop a plan to get back on track. The outline for this approach is Drucker's book "The Five Most Important Questions You Will Ever Ask About Your Organization". Although it sounds simple, the approach is very thought-provoking and worth every minute of time you put towards it.

Why Aren't We Performing Like We Should?

Managers often get the feeling their organization's performance just isn't what it should be, and can't put a finger on why not. It's a frustrating feeling for everyone involved – the manager, the employees, and the end customer.

Business performance is a measurable thing. Typically, managers measure key metrics in one or more of four categories – cost, time (schedule), quality, and scope (determined by the size of a project or production run). Performance in one category influences the others in one way or the other – if you want something done quickly, the quality and/or scope may suffer; and if you want something done well, the cost will generally rise. Metrics are the indicators of performance, but not the critical driver or cause. These measurements only indicate the degree of success relative to set goals.

A general organizational framework addresses the four basic components of any organization – infrastructure, processes, technology, and people. In the world of management improvement, organizations may employ proven methods to become more efficient by taking a hard look at many of these areas. Notably, an organization may use the "Lean" and "Six Sigma" processes (among others) to minimize waste and improve the quality of a product. These methods may treat the symptoms of the problem rather than the most critical issue.

It's worth noting that the people component of the framework influences the other three organizational components. In other words, it's the people who decide what technology, infrastructure, and processes are best for what you are doing. So, a key to success is to have the right people in the right places within the organization (see Jim Collins' book

"Good to Great"). The most important key is knowing how to treat them.

For example, I witnessed this comment told to a seasoned leader by the leader's boss: "You need to change your management style so your employees fear for their jobs – you'll get more out of them".

In a different organization, I overheard an employee respond to his supervisor when asked to get something accomplished: "I'll give it my best". The supervisor's response was: "I don't want your best, I want it done".

Both of these examples indicate the type of leadership culture in those organizations – neither of which instills a positive work environment. Leadership as a practice means how the bosses influence the attitudes of the employees to achieve goals. The more positive the leadership, the better performance you get. Although there are circumstances where a "command and control" style is useful (the Marines who need to charge an objective or firefighters during an emergency). A business setting usually is not one of them.

The Bottom Line - Leadership is Critical

Peter Drucker, considered the father of modern management, separated business practice into the components of "management" and "leadership". With that in mind, he considered himself in the people business as opposed to the metrics business – indicating people make the business work, and effective leadership is critical. Considering that 70% of people who leave their company leave because of their immediate supervisor (supported by multiple polls by the Gallup and others), learning effective leadership skills should be on the top of any supervisor's list. Many books and theories are available to learn about ways to achieve success (for a good start, see the book called "Primal Leadership" by Daniel Goleman and others). The point is to create a positive working environment where the employees feel part of the team. Think of your employees like volunteers - because they are.

What To Do About A Poor Manager

A previous boss of mine emerged out of his office shouting "everyone, stop the 'xxxx' process – it's broke and you need to fix it". Of course, we proceeded to fix the problem, which turned out to be more of a perception than reality. At first, we, the staff, thought the boss discovered a real issue. Then, the next week the boss found another anomaly and again, rushed out of his office in an uproar. And, as concerned employees do, we all stopped what we were doing to focus on this issue. The problem was this became a routine event - each week the boss would declare an emergency and we all would rush to investigate the issue. Eventually, it became the "panic of the week" and an expectation. The problem was we had to plan on disrupting our normal schedule to focus on an imagined problem.

This was the same boss who gave me an annual performance evaluation of "exceeds expectations" and within a month told me I don't get results. This same boss gave me his "golden nugget" of leadership advice by telling me I needed to change my style to where my staff feared for their jobs so they would perform better. Needless to say, he and I had differences of opinion on how to lead.

My intent is not to whine (although that does seem appropriate) – it's to demonstrate the leadership problem. I hope it's clear that this particular boss significantly lacked effective leadership skills. In my view, he remained a theory X kind of guy (thinking you have to beat employees into submission to get results) while most of the business world focused on theory Y (where bosses respect people and the value they bring to the table) – see Douglas McGregor's writing on theory X/Y.

Although I saw my previous boss as the immediate issue, I have since realized he was not the biggest problem. I realized someone 1) put my boss there, 2) failed to evaluate his leadership skills, and 3) tolerated his behavior. Could it be his boss did not understand what effective leadership looked like, or didn't pay attention, or worse – didn't care? In the end, I eventually left my boss and the company (recall the saying: people join a company, but leave their boss).

So, what are you to do?

First, take a look at those who put your ineffective boss in place. Do they seem to understand that there is a problem and can recognize poor leadership when they see it? If not, it's not going to improve much so it may be time to start looking for a better place to work. During your interviews see if you can discover who your boss might be and assess the leadership capability, which is not always an easy task. If they seem to understand and care about the organization's productivity, provide them feedback on the issues of concern. Upper management should feel compelled to remove ineffective bosses since they create high turnover rates (a big cost to the bottom line) and lack of employee commitment to the organization (see the book "The No Asshole Rule" by Robert Sutton). In addition, keeping the ineffective boss in a position for which they have little talent is not fair to them (having to do a job they are not particularly good at or ill-prepared) or their employees (who have to suffer the brunt of poor leadership).

Second, prepare yourself to be a great boss. Learn about the difference between "managing" and "leading" and why it matters – because it really does. Things are managed and people are led. Managing is linked to metrics – behaviors and emotions are linked to leading (see "Primal Leadership" by

Goleman and others for a good starting point). An article in the Harvard Business Review noted that most who are put into leadership positions typically are not provided the appropriate education and training until years later. So, don't wait – start now to learn what effective leadership looks like before you are asked to lead.

People Behave Based on How They Are Treated

You never know how your treatment of others impacts their lives. A recent data shows less than 35% of employees are engaged at work. Other studies demonstrate approximately 70% of those who voluntarily leave a job do so because of the immediate supervisor. The data implies the treatment and leadership of staff are critically important. One definition defines leadership as an influence on a person's behavior. In that regard, everyone possesses a degree of leadership although many don't realize it. Others may realize the influence they have and choose not to use it well which is a problem. Some use leadership for the overall good of the organization realizing some difficult choices are necessary. Let me explain. Those in a position of power, like supervisors and managers, wield influence in important ways. Managers must realize those who report to them, either as employees or contractors, have a certain level of stress or hidden fear of doing something wrong in the eyes of the manager. The manager drives the stress or fear in two ways – clarity in setting expectations and response to things that don't go well for reasons other than intentional insubordination.

Leaders Need to Take Action

A critical responsibility for the manager involves taking action on those who create havoc. I witnessed supervisors who treated their employees as if they were stupid and were allowed to do so by upper management. I also witnessed organizations who knew managers were dysfunctional creating a poor working environment for all but elected to keep them in place. In this particular case, the organization's upper management elected to keep the dysfunctional manager in place for training purposes. The message sent to the rest of the organization is less than good – the organization doesn't care how the employees/contractors are treated or don't have the fortitude to take the necessary action. In either case, the morale and performance of the working force are reduced, not to mention the respect for the managers as well.

The message for managers is this: think about how you use influence at the individual as well as the organizational level. Everything you do and say, or not do or not say, is an influence. Know that everyone is watching you at all times to see what you choose to do or not do. Your treatment of others has an impact – so it's up to you to know what kind of impact that should be.

The Basics of Running the Office

"What staff meeting? What do you mean?"

This was the response for each time I asked about it after taking over as the boss in four organizations. My prior experience primarily involved large organizations with many moving parts. The organizations I worked for provided great exposure to many types of managerial and leadership training events. I was even fortunate to take a class from Dr. Edward Deming, who was affiliated with the Total Quality Management movement many years ago.

Subsequently, I learned about the works of several other pillars in the field – people such as Peter Drucker (the father of modern management), Warren Bennis, and others. Based on all of this exposure, I developed a set of practices that seem to work.

First, there is no single best way to run an organization – because there are just too many variables to pick just one. The variables include you, the boss, the nature of the work environment, and the nature of the employees. My advice is to be cautious of articles starting with "The 7 Key Things Great Leaders Do" or something like that. Management is just not that simple to be boiled down to 7 key things or 5 greatest attributes of leadership, or whatever…If it were that simple, we would not need the thousands of books on the topic or a large number of MBA's in the workforce.

That said, I firmly believe a few fundamentals exist:

- Select your staff for their strengths and make their weaknesses irrelevant (this is a Drucker-ism). Do not hire your buddies, your family members, or others unless they are the right fit – period.

- Focus your staff on the organization's higher purpose – and it's not growth or profit margin. It has to be genuine, meaningful, and the truth.

- Pay the employees fairly and treat them as if they were volunteers – because they are (another Drucker-ism).

- Create an organizational execution plan with your team to create goals, schedules, and quality/cost targets as if it was all project management – because it is.

And then, start having recurring staff meetings so you can –

- Find out how you can help your staff achieve the goals.
- Get the staff to collaborate as a team to achieve the higher organizational purpose.
- Develop trust within the organization so you all can live full lives.

Why Do We Have So Many Job-Hoppers?

The title reflects a question I saw on Linkedin a few months ago from a member of a corporate human resources department. I replied to the question with a rationale that may help in understanding the new dynamics of the corporate hiring.

Point 1 – In this new era of the "knowledge worker" (otherwise known as an IT professional), the means of production is no longer at the company like was in the manufacturing era. It's now in the heads of the knowledge workers.

Point 2 – Knowledge workers (the means of production) are transportable and to a large degree interchangeable. Certain IT skill sets can generally be used in multiple companies with minimal re-training. I once overheard a conversation by some IT workers about what company they had been with recently and where they might go next – as if it was a certainty. This occurred at a corporate "beer-bash", one of the perks geared to keep employees.

Point 3 – The corporate perks in the knowledge worker world are commonplace and probably make little difference. One of the staff members at a tech company asked why the company puts on the beer-bashes saying it's a waste of money. I told them this company does it because the company across the street does it, as does Google, as does…(fill in the blank).

Point 4 - The corporate world is more concerned about what Wall Street thinks in the short term than the fate of employees in the long term. Hardly a day goes by without a news report of a corporate "downsizing" because the company didn't meet the projected quarterly revenue numbers. To balance the books, companies lay off X-number of employees who were once highly sought-after.

Point 5 (this is the big one) – Recent polls by Gallup and other organizations indicate the level of engaged employees (workers committed to the company) is about 30 percent, meaning 70 percent are neutral (don't care either way) or actively disengaged (really unhappy). Other data indicates most employees (70 percent or so) leave a company due to the behavior of their immediate supervisor. Recall the saying that "people join companies and leave bosses".

Considering the points outlined above, is there any wonder why there are so many job-hoppers?

So, what's the message to the organizations?

- Focus on learning what "leadership" really is and teach it to the supervisors and project managers. Shift the role of the manager to one of leading and less on technical skills.

- Find a "real" higher purpose for the company so employees feel connected to their work. Purpose is not measured in "profit" or "growth".

- Consider increasing productivity through better leadership/management as opposed to having to cut cost with layoffs. It's not that hard to do if you understand what leadership/management really means.

Job-hoppers/employees will stay longer if they believe you and corporate management really care.

Now You're the Boss – Short Pointers

Adjust your time. Did you ever wish you had more "face time" with the boss before you became one? Now that you hold a leadership position, do you wonder how your boss ever found the time to give you? Should your use of time change now that you're in charge of some folks? The answer is – you bet it changes!

As a boss, your priorities and focus changes since you now oversee a staff. A boss continues to look at tasks in a similar fashion as a staff member but from a different perspective. One still categorizes tasks in four basic areas according to author Stephen Covey: important and urgent, important but not urgent, not important but urgent, and not important and not urgent. Defining your tasks into the correct category provides the best clues as to what to do first.

The terms important and urgent relate to your position. An urgent task needs attention sooner than others – in different terms, it will get you yelled at first if not done on time. For instance, as a boss, resolving a personnel issue quickly before it disrupts the rest of the staff is urgent. A staff member would not even think to add this to the task list as urgent or otherwise.

An important task refers to what your boss says. If a task relates to the bosses' agenda, then it's important. If it relates to your staff succeeding, then it's important. If it affects the goals and objectives of the unit, then it's important. If the task is like any of these criteria, and the deadline is soon with lots to be done, then it's urgent and important.

For example (and this equates to a pet peeve), consider the situation of you and a staff member meeting in your office and the phone rings. Most people believe answering the phone is both urgent and important when, in fact, it's neither. In addition, by answering this type of call you're telling your staff member that the unknown call is more important than the "face time" he or she is getting with the boss – not a good signal to send.

However, if you know a key phone call (important and urgent information) is due in any minute, you must pre-warn your guest that you may have to be interrupted during your meeting. Or, if the call comes in, excuse yourself and explain quickly the importance of the call and take it.

So, what does a boss add to the calendar that staff members don't? In short, time with the staff. Just as parents must make time for their kids, bosses must make time available for the staff, and peers for coordinating supporting activities. Block out time to provide guidance (staff meetings, project reviews, etc.), and support (attendance at key meetings with staff members). Make time to visit the workspace – being visible and accessible. Generally, this staff time takes the form of "how can I support you" versus "this is how to do your job". It's team building time.

Staff time on your calendar competes with other tasks (usually boss assigned) that you must get done. The four categories mentioned above come into play when deciding what comes first. Your staff pulls on your time just as your boss does. If this happens, look to delegate some tasks. Accomplishing all of what you think you need to do may not work. Passing some off, or dropping those less important tasks may suffice (or just say no to some). If you really need help deciding, discuss it with your boss especially if your tasks exceed your available time. Try to keep as much staff time as possible or practical. Time with your staff provides more positive impact than most items on your calendar.

Be Clear. Remember the last time you thought to take the initiative on a key topic only to discover others also took it upon themselves to act? Or, you chose not to act because the last time you did so your boss fussed at you? Or, you failed to act when they expected you to, but you didn't know it was your responsibility?

The role of the boss includes clarifying roles and responsibilities. In many cases, the organizational chart identifies the broad responsibilities. For example, in a typical facility maintenance organization, the HVAC (heating, ventilating, and air conditioning) folks complete the HVAC work. The gray area becomes the electrical and controls work associated with HVAC activities. Some organizations require certain staff to complete these duties while other organizations allow the HVAC staff to complete minor tasks outside the HVAC traditional work. Organizational charts fail to cover the definitive separation in where there could be overlap. This clarification relies on the boss.

How the issues become clarified may affect the employees. I witnessed a senior leader scold one of my subordinates for taking the initiative in resolving an internal customer service issue. Our boss consistently requested we maintain the "corporate" vehicle in a timely fashion. Our primary issue focused on obtaining a car key to allow us to accomplish our task. The subordinate finally decided to make a copy of the car key so we would not have to beg for one in the future. The senior leader fussed at her for obtaining the key without special permission. In the end, we obtained a key to allow us to accomplish the task assigned by the senior leader. However, the employee failed to take the initiative again and retired a few years later – much sooner than expected.

You as the boss need to decide in broad terms which person or group owns which responsibility. You also need to initiate discussions between those affected parties where gray areas exist. With your oversight, they determine where the lines of separation lie. That way, they buy into the roles and gain clarity on their duties.

Uncertainty and failure to provide clarity in responsibility greatly hinder success. During periods of uncertainty, people fail to act or freeze in place by thinking others may own the task. In other cases, people fear taking action unless the organization clearly identified the task as their responsibility.

Make sure you understand your place in the organization – your roles and responsibilities. Then, as the boss, you make sure the staff understands their roles and responsibilities. Discuss the topic openly with the staff. Sometimes they may suggest a role change that makes perfect sense for the situation. If the staff fails to act, the problem may not rest with them – it might rest with you, the boss. Make certain you provide clarity.

Check your C's. Can you recall the bosses you worked for over the years? No doubt some stood out while others you might consider less than perfect for the position. Consider what makes some bosses better than others. After your review, think about what makes you a better candidate to move up the ladder.

In church this past Sunday, the senior pastor preached on the personal qualities of competence and character (therefore, the "C's"). Though his focus centered on faith, the two characteristics fit well in the leadership arena. In different terms, these may be translated as technical know-how and people skills.

By way of definition, I see technical skills as the knowledge of how to accomplish a skill or task. It's simple – you can wire a circuit, build a house, design furniture, or not. How well one does that is a matter of degree. For instance, I can design furniture for a corporate headquarters, just not very well. Some folks possess more talent than others in a particular area. That talent makes them valuable and therefore thought of as more competent in that area.

In contrast to your skills and talents, how you represent yourself defines your character. Interpret character as values, integrity, honesty, morals, and the like. These also come in degrees. Some people possess a stronger sense of "character" than others, similar to possessing a degree of technical competence. How people perceive your character defines your success in leading them. Why is that?

One of my graduate professors stated, "to lead you need only ten percent technical know-how and ninety percent people skills". He means it takes less technical competency and more leadership talent to be the boss. This statement implies leadership equates to a talent in and of itself – like plumbing, cabinet making or computer programming.

The concept now becomes a sliding scale on what a boss needs – how much of one talent versus the other. If given the choice, in what areas would you want your boss to be good? I prefer one who possesses the ability to motivate and treat people right; someone who looks long-term and not just for the short-term performance; someone who provides guidance, sets goals and who knows how to involve the staff in those efforts; and someone who realizes these activities are part of the leadership role. I prefer not to work for a very good technician. I can learn the technical skills from a school.

This brings us to the topic of "character". Assuming you agree that leadership may be defined as influence, a leader lacks influence if those to be led lack confidence in the leader. They need to believe in him and trust his judgment. Trust needs to be there. It won't be if the leader lacks character as defined above.

The Texas Tech basketball coach Bobby Knight provides a good example on this issue. No doubt he possesses the technical skills to teach the sport. However, he seriously lacks the self-control and apparently the long-term concern for his players. Otherwise, he wouldn't scream at or embarrass his players in public. You may have heard of his chair throwing episodes during televised games. His style, in my view, motivates by fear and gets short-term results. But, he sets an incredibly poor example for his players and assistant coaches on leadership. I doubt few say to themselves after seeing one of his temper tantrums "I wish I could be just like coach Knight".

So, the choice becomes technical competence or character. But, why choose – why not have both? To be a boss, you must possess the characteristics to be trusted, pay attention to people issues and topics, and be willing to take the tough actions (discipline). Technical skills help (enough is needed to be able to recognize a problem), but most plumbers want guidance and support in the front office, not another good plumber. When selected to be the boss, change your area of competency – move from technical to leadership. The other "C", character, becomes the focus and hopefully the reason they picked you.

Imagine. Remember thinking how well your group performed on that important project when everything clicked? Recall that the right people showed up and made the right decisions and it just felt right? Can you imagine that happening all the time?

As you think about your operation, your staff, equipment, tools, and support, imagine what it would take to make it really good. What about really great? What would you, as the boss, need to do to achieve such a team?

We all need the tools to do our jobs. Imagine your company acquiring the right equipment to make your team extremely productive. Is the additional investment that much more in the long run than what you usually get?

We must set up procedures and processes with those groups that affect our product. Think about the collaboration required to get it absolutely right and not just for you – for the good of the company. Is the effort that difficult to start?

Imagine the ideal staff - well trained, capable and enthusiastic about working for you.

Many bosses envision their ideal situation over and over, year after year with little to no improvement. Some organizations, however, actually achieve their goal. They acquire all the right things to excel. How do they do that?

The book, "In Search of Excellence" includes a story about a group of CEO's reviewing the McDonald's operations when they led all others in their industry. The group discovered no magic in McDonald's processes and operations. The revelation was simple – any company could execute their business the McDonald's way. The difference was McDonald's did it. They executed. They performed. They achieved incredible success.

So, what constitutes the key ingredient for you as the boss? In a single word – Courage.

Coach Krzyzewski (K), the famous basketball coach for Duke defines courage as "daring to do what you imagine" (see his book "Beyond Basketball").

Put into action in our context, it means asking for the right budget to get the needed training, the right tools, and the right staff. It includes stepping out of your comfort zone to figure out the correct process and procedures with your peers.

And, here's the hard part for many, it means ending up with the right staff. This implies assessing the current staff's ability, keeping those who fit and moving those who don't elsewhere. Your staff affects everything you do and produce – they equate to the critical component of any organization.

Many bosses fear the personnel part of their jobs. The key here focuses on the strengths of each person. Sometimes those who possess few strengths in your process may fit great in someone else's. It's fair for you and them to find the right spot to take advantage of those strengths.

Imagine what it takes to make your organization great. Then find the courage to make the changes to get there. It involves selling your ideas to upper management which may not always succeed. It includes finding a better fitting job for some of your staff. In reality, you, your staff and company deserve it.

Keep your cool. Do you gauge how your day will go based on how your boss feels? Have you watched the faces of employees when their unpredictable boss enters the room? Do they all hold their breath to see which way the wind is blowing that day? Are stomach knots a part of each day when you have to see your boss because you don't know if he's going to be Jekyll or Hyde?

I recall the cop movies during the 80's when the detective, Dirty Harry, went to see his boss who then began a constant barrage of yelling. Of course, the detective held his ground and at times yelled back. It seemed that all police captains during that era had a leadership issue. Though this added to the setup of the story it also adds to the point I intend to make.

Employees like consistency. They want to know what to expect. Otherwise, they freeze in fear of doing the wrong thing. If the boss likes an activity accomplished one way when he, or she, is feeling fine, but another way when disgruntled, how is the employee to know what to do? Employees need to know what to expect so they know how to perform.

So, how do you as the boss control this situation? Easy. Keep your cool. Be consistent with how employees perceive you. React the same regardless of how you feel. They don't care, or know, that your favorite team lost the big game last night. Or that your child created mass hysteria at the house. Or whatever it was that set your attitude. In any case, it doesn't matter. It does matter that you, as the boss, set the tone that best suits the environment in which the best work is done.

A four-star general once told his subordinate commanders if they lost their cool during peacetime, what would make him think they could keep it during a war. He told them to maintain a level head at all times – to be consistent.

This does not mean the tone should not change. Indeed, it may vary quite a bit depending on the activity you need to perform, or the environment you need to create to achieve the greatest performance. Make change based on the need versus your personal situation. For example, you expect the local fire chief to change the tone of the station based on an alarm. When the alarm sounds, the chief's attitude immediately changes as does that of the firefighters. The chief needs to instill a sense of urgency in the crew so the tone changes as you expect it would. If not, lives could be at stake.

If you enter your office as the boss in a nasty mood, expect your employees to sense it and react accordingly. Production drops and attitudes develop. If you enter your office with calm, as if you know exactly what you are doing, production and morale improve. Employees sense your confidence and act accordingly.

A Gallup poll revealed that the single most important factor in employee retention and satisfaction is the immediate boss – you. Your attitude affects your office much like it affects your family. I witnessed a complete change in the performance of a unit just by a change in leadership. How you come across sets the tone and attitudes of everyone in the office. Be aware of what sets your attitude and control how employees perceive you. Keep your cool.

Learn about people. Do you wonder what makes some organizations successful and effective and others not? Have you compared the skills of the staff for various groups to find no single difference in ability, yet some succeed more than others? Have you hit the bookstores to find the "secret" to leadership and been mesmerized by the huge quantity of advice?

Successful leaders create effective organizations by making the most of what's available to them. They learn how to optimize the tools of the job as defined as facilities, software, and the like. Great leaders know how to maximize the funds provided to them by learning the budget language and the system by which funds are provided. Once senior leadership figures out who uses the tools and funds well, they tend to increase those budgets.

Leaders use the tools and budgets as a means to an end. Their secret is in how they use those means. In fact, they don't use them much at all. Instead, they entice their staffs to make the most of what they have. So, the big secret lies in how they motivate the staff.

Bookstores line their shelves with numerous business and management books that address every possible aspect of running a business or organization. Over the many years, management gurus have offered multiple methods to create success – Management by Objectives (MBO), Total Quality Management (TQM), and others. Many of the approaches work to some degree. What these approaches lack is the "how" in employee motivation.

I grant you the bookstores include volumes on motivation as well. I found one book as the single most influential book for millions of people over the decades. The principles covered in the book address how to "handle" people in general and apply to employees as well as others. In effect, the author covers how a person might influence another to his way of thinking, or in other terms, how to get into someone's head.

For example, one chapter describes how to gain the favor of those you want on your side. The author says to find a common interest and talk about that before discussing any business. If the person you want on your side plays a particular sport, find some information on that sport and casually mention it. Or, while in the office of this target person, find something in the office you can speak sincerely about.

Another chapter points out the words everyone wants to hear. In dealing with employees, especially in public, they love to hear their name. Everyone does. The praise that goes with it must be genuine and sincere, and you must get the name correct.

Dale Carnegie wrote this book of "secrets" and made a great success out of the principles. He called the book "How to Win Friends and Influence People", written in 1936. Though the book initially focused on salespeople, the ideas apply universally.

If you rush out to get the book, avoid the new version by the Dale Carnegie Institute – I don't think it's as good. Find the original version. Read it and learn how to sincerely motivate (and not manipulate) people to create a successful and supportive environment for your staff.

Learn the language. In my travels overseas I recall attempting to speak to the locals only to get the deer in the headlights effect. One danger in trying to speak their language is they speak back – another deer in the headlights moment, but in reverse. I once asked the time of a German citizen in

Bavaria. I apparently was successful in making myself understood because he replied in very clear German, none of which I understood. I simply nodded my head as if I had a clue what he said.

Not all leaders come with the complete technical background required to be conversant with those being led. Technical talent comes in second to leadership skill, but it helps to have some to mix in with the team. Understanding the jargon brings you closer to the fold so to speak. Acquiring, or demonstrating technical ability adds to the boss's credibility.

So, what constitutes learning the language, or what at least helps? In short, getting some sort of qualification or certification. I found nearly every functional area offers some sort of "stamp on the forehead" that says you possess some ability to do the job. Many functional areas provide several levels of certification. Typically, there exists an entry or training level as well as a fully qualified level. Licenses come in levels from apprentice to fully qualified, such as in the construction trades. Engineers use a training designation until they gain certain time on the job under a fully licensed "professional engineer", or PE.

Does a license or certification make you better technically? Is a PE any better of an engineer with or without the designation? Not really from an education point of view. However, the certification brings credibility to the position and a certain confidence level with others (peers, subordinates, and senior leadership). It demonstrates a clear understanding of the function. I feel much safer knowing I work in a building built and designed by a registered engineer or architect.

For a new boss, obtaining a certification demonstrates a commitment to those you supervise. Subordinates appreciate your willingness to learn their business, especially if you come from a functional area outside of theirs. In addition, achieving some sort of credentials allows you to understand the jargon used in the daily business life.

On the other hand, some people exist just to collect titles and letters to put after their name on the business card. They desire to appear qualified which is why you always need to conduct an interview before you hire them. The title collectors most of the time emerge after a conversation or two. That is not to say those with many certifications are unprofessional. You have to determine which is which.

As a boss must you get certified? No. Would it benefit you as a leader? Absolutely. Would it help you gain respect and credibility? Without a doubt. Bottom line: consider getting your certification.

Manage your mentality. Remember that time your boss "helped" you with a process that you quite didn't understand by doing it for you? Recall how you felt when you still didn't understand it after the boss's help? Didn't you wish they provided more training and development time so the boss didn't have to help in that way?

As a boss, one of your many tasks includes training your staff to perform using processes, systems, and equipment. Sometimes these items fail to work as needed and require adjustments. The questions now become who's task is it to accomplish the adjustments – and why.

Edward Deming, one of the authors of the Total Quality Management (TQM) movement (though he did not like the TQM term), stated the best person to "manage" the process, or system is the one using it. Based on his approach, the ones to make the adjustment would be the employees themselves. So, what's a new boss to do knowing the employee probably won't get it right or finish it on time?

The answer becomes easy if you want to retain good staff. The boss needs to allow employees to manage processes and systems with the appropriate guidance. In effect, you as the boss delegate this task to those who understand the process best. You give them the desired results and limiting factors (constraints) and a timeline which they need to meet. Then, you let them do it and accept their product as their first draft or a perfectly operable system.

Many a new boss desires to just take over the task and do it himself. By doing so, the boss misses a great opportunity to provide training to the staff, takes up valuable time doing something others can do, and shows a lack of confidence in the employees. All of these things are less than good. New bosses need to avoid what I call the "Takeover Mentality".

Protect your feet. Don't you just hate it when one of your peers embarrasses you in front of the boss in a big meeting? When they tell everyone that you're the cause of the holdup, yet you had no clue? Especially when they had every chance in the world to tell you in plenty of time to get the issue fixed before the meeting? Don't you just hate that, and don't you want to get them back?

My advice – take the high road and show them how to do it properly. Making yourself look good at the expense of others is like loading a gun and blowing off your own feet. By taking unfair advantage of others you create more issues with those with whom you need to work (maybe not now, but just you wait). In addition, if you happen to work with a perceptive boss, that foot damage will be detected anyway. A good boss looks for team players, not individual heroes.

To keep from blowing off your feet at a meeting, consider a couple of things well before the meeting:

-   Who else on the team needs to know what you know? When you come across what may be key information, think through the organization chart to determine who might benefit from learning what you know.

- Look at any project with the big picture in mind to see if you discover something others may have missed. You may focus only on your area, but the boss wants the entire project done - not just your part.

- Let others know of their issues in private and in plenty of time to do something about them before being embarrassed in a meeting. They'll thank you for it and hopefully will help you when you desperately need it.

I once witnessed a lead project participant brief a team of high-level leaders and other staff working to resolve issues on a huge (and I mean huge) contract. He informed the leaders that the maintenance group needed to fix some signage in a key facility. Though the leaders needed to know that information, the participant would have been better served by telling the action person well before the meeting, and in private. Not only that, the person doing the briefing asked for the original signs to be put up in the first place. In the spirit of this section, the participant took aim at both feet at once.

The maintenance guys fixed the signs after staying silent at the meeting. The "big boss" of the company clearly displayed signs of displeasure. After the meeting, I found out the source of displeasure resided with the person "ratting" on his team members. As it turned out the big boss happened to know the source of the original signs and realized immediately what happened in the meeting.

Avoid blowing off your feet by employing teamwork and some smart coordination. Share information sooner rather than later. Look at the big picture with the intent of a successful team working on a successful project. Share embarrassing information in private with your peers and subordinates. The big bosses probably learned these lessons already, which may have helped them in their success.

In summary, avoid focusing on you looking good at someone else's expense. If you help in the success of the team, the project, and the company, the boss will notice. If you don't help, the boss will notice that too.

Recognize anyone? Do you remember the time you accomplished a great thing and no one else noticed? Remember the time the person in the next workstation received an award for just doing his job? What about the time one of your peers gained recognition in a big ceremony but failed to show up – what was that all about?

As a new boss (or at least a potential one) your job includes the decision to incorporate a recognition program. So, why do one? Why not? What's your goal or purpose for going through the effort? If you decide to initiate (or continue) a program, what considerations should you include?

Everyone likes to be recognized for accomplishments. This summer at the local pool you no doubt heard some child call to the parents "look at me, look at me" followed by parental praise. And surely the last time you received a promotion you called a significant person in your life (parent, spouse or significant other) to relay the good news. We all like praise and thanks for a job well done.

The purpose of a recognition program centers on morale building. The sole reason an employee receives an award relates to the level of contribution – it's the "look at me" syndrome. As you think back to watching those who received an award, I suspect you felt a sense of envy or at least a desire to do better. That's the target of the program – to recognize those who contribute in an exceptional manner and encourage others to aspire to higher levels of performance.

Initiating a program takes great thought. First, publish a set of criteria and stick to it. Choose criteria that employees must stretch to achieve so they truly accomplish something. Second, the award must be sincere – avoid giving an award to the next person in line. Doing so dilutes the value of the award. If no one really meets the criteria, choose not to give out the award. Third, decide how to recognize the person. Pick a meaningful award that means something to the employee. Some prefer money while others prefer time off. Either way, their name must be advertised on some list or plaque for bragging rights to their loved ones.

In addition, the venue is important. Shy employees may prefer a small event while others want you to invite everyone they know. Some would love to see family members present while others want only peers. If the morale of the employee is your purpose, then find out what is meaningful to that employee and try to accommodate the need.

As a precaution, be careful of the criteria you select. What you state there, in a sense, becomes performance criteria. Your criteria must reflect what you value in your business. For example, meeting sales goals ethically is far better than meeting them at any cost assuming you intend to be in business for the long haul.

In my opinion, a recognition program absolutely increases morale if correctly executed. Make it sincere and reflect business values. Make it meaningful to the successful award winner by presenting something of importance in the correct venue. And be sure to correctly say the most important words during the ceremony – the winner's name.

Manage expectations. Have you noticed your work ethic exceeds everyone else's? I'm sure you have wondered how some people get away with doing so little. What about the people who appear to be the bosses' favorite and get the rewards without performing? How can the workplace operate like this – why don't they understand?

Consider the idea that everyone thinks they do a great job. Don't you believe you do a wonderful job? If this, in fact, is the case, then what drives people to perform at different levels?

This weekend the local newspaper featured an article about a company that recently changed owners. The previous leadership guided the company from overseas. The employees felt left out of any decision-making process and isolated. In effect, they were unsure how to perform.

The new owners reside locally and maintain a presence on the premises. Employees enjoy open access to leadership that includes the employees in the business process. The difference between the old and new management systems seems obvious – it's how leadership treated the employees. As much as I agree with that, I think it goes deeper.

Including the employees in the business process clearly added a great deal to the morale of the employees. These employees believed they did a great job under the old leadership. They now think they perform well under the new leadership. The difference lies with what the employees "think" management expects from them. I suspect the employees received little guidance with the old management team. The new team allows the employees the freedom to participate in the business, therefore learning first-hand what they need to do. Where expectations may not have been so clear in the past, the employees understand what needs to be done with the new system.

Overall, two changes took place in this company. First, a participative leadership team took over. Second, employees gained a clear idea of what the company expected from them by way of the participation. The end result created a win-win situation for the company.

So, what improvement resulted? In 2003 the old company reported a loss of $426 million (before taxes) on sales of $739 million. After the change to the new leadership, the company increased the workforce by 280 persons and still generated $1 billion in revenue in 2005.

I grant the solution probably entailed more than what I portrayed. My point centers on the expectations of the employees. Generally, everyone wants to do a good job and everyone believes they achieve that. Leadership must ensure employees understand what defines a good job. Leadership owns the role of establishing the expectations. With a void here, employees work to their own set of expectations which may not match the needs of the company.

As a new boss, make sure your employees know what you expect. Ask your employees if you feel uncertain or unclear about what they understand. Ask your boss if you feel unclear about what is expected of you. Performance must match expectations to create success which we desire for our employees and ourselves.

Manage your projects. Count the number of times you heard the term "project management" in the past few months. Do you know what that means? Some folks carry the title Project Manager and remain unclear about the tasks involved. Others claim to do project management and possess little to no knowledge of what that entails.

A new leader may end up responsible for many projects. The term project manager implies managing things versus leading people. In fact, both talents – managing and leadership – become co-mingled. You, as the boss, lead those people who support the functions and tasks that you manage. You may even lead several project managers who lead others in support of their projects.

The four basic elements managed throughout a project include:

- *Scope:* The requirements as dictated by the customer (internal or external). For facility managers, typically scope relates to construction or renovation projects. The customer relates what the business unit needs as an end product. The manager must start with a clear definition and obtain the agreement of the customer. It becomes difficult to measure success with a fuzzy scope definition.

-       *Schedule:* The time factors of tasks involved with the scope (timetable, PERT chart, production schedule). Normally, a schedule pertains to the tasks involved in completing the scope of work. Numerous software packages provide a means to chart these tasks. Every manager needs the single most critical milestone – the overall need date from the customer. Customers define this as the date they become operational.

-       *Cost:* Cost relates to budget or production or savings achieved. Normally this entails the overall costs of completing the construction tasks to achieve the scope requirements. The manager compares the costs to the given budget.

-       *Quality:* The quality of the project, in materials, labor or processes used, directly influences the cost, schedule, and scope. Customers may choose to not accept a higher quality product due to the cost, or the time it takes to achieve a final product (schedule), or it exceeds their needs (scope).

Managing includes measuring. The manager gathers the support team to review on a recurring basis progress in each of the above-mentioned areas. For scope, the team reviews the scope to make sure the final product meets the needs as defined by the customer. The team compares the tasks on the projected schedule with actual events to ensure the completion date meets the needs of the customer. The running costs get compared to the estimates to avoid cost overruns. The team tracks the quality to make sure it meets the needs as defined by the scope, is affordable (in line with the estimates) and meets the schedule.

The project manager owns the title of the most critical factor in the project's success. Every team member must run all activities through the project manager – everything. The manager provides the single overall view of the project and how each team member's role affects the others. Hiring a strong leader in this role makes or breaks a project.

Leadership plays a critical part of every managed project. As noted, the project manager manages the things involved in a project – scope, schedule, cost, and quality. People accomplish these "things" and therefore need leadership. How well a boss leads the team determines the attitudes of the members and therefore the success of each element. The boss leads the team and manages the project. In project management, leadership and management co-exist and depend on each other. Great project managers, much like great leaders, excel in people skills.

Boss or coach? Remember hearing about the huge earnings the big companies acquired and wondered how they accomplished that? Did you wonder if the company structure and processes led to the success, or if management got the credit? And if management did it, what did they actually do to deserve the praise? What does management do to succeed?

Part of the answer relates to the same factor that makes a sports team perform well – the coach. In one sense, a coach acts much like a boss by providing similar things. He (or she) brings strategy, tools (such as teaching skills), and expertise (knowledge). The better coaches know how to pass these along to the players and, more importantly, how to keep the team focused on them.

Recently, one of my kids' teams won the city basketball championship – what I call a success. This team uses a head and assistant coach with significantly different styles. During the season, and especially in the championship game, the assistant coach focused on what the team did poorly. He typically began his comments with what the players failed to execute well. In fact, he and his son got into a heated discussion about what the boy needed to do better. They continued this conversation while the rest of the team played.

The head coach immediately realized the impact of the assistant's actions. The players' attitudes and mindset diminished and began to alter how they played. He called a timeout and told the assistant to let him be the only one to speak at this point. The head coach told the players two things – keep their heads in the game (no distractions), and that their performance exceeded his expectations.

These coaches sat at either end of the bench. Their ability to motivate equated to a similar difference – two ends of the spectrum. Where one focused on the negative in hopes he could "shame" the players into playing better, the other took the high road. Where one caused the players to look down when he spoke, the other had eye contact. The spirit of the players could not have swung any more extreme during this episode.

The differences in these coaches explain why some achieve success and others miss the mark. With all things equal, the one who "manages" attitudes well succeed. The head coach (boss) knew his players (employees) respond, like most of us, to positive and constructive advice. He knew how to maintain the mindset required to keep up performance.

My point in saying all of this relates back to the success of companies. As good as the processes, procedures, and structure might be, without the leadership in a coaching role success may still be elusive. In fact, poor leadership and lack of coaching nearly guarantee limited performance. After all, it's not the processes or structure that gets things accomplished – it's the people (players).

The next time you read about the success of a company, look to see how they coach the team. Are the leaders the Jack Welsh type (of General Electric fame), or something much less? In different terms (and those of you who played organized sports with a coach relate to this idea well), would you want to play for a Bobby Knight (a coach with an attitude) or a Coach K (of Duke fame)/Coach Williams (of UNC fame)? You as the boss need to learn to coach.

By the way, my team won by 13 points!

References

Altmäe, S., Türk, K., & Ott-Siim Toomet. (2013). Thomas-Kilmann's conflict management modes and their relationship to Fiedler's leadership styles (basing on Estonian organizations). *Baltic Journal of Management, 8*, 45-65. doi:10.1108/17465261311291650

Anantatmula, V. S. (2010). Project manager leadership role in improving project performance. *Engineering Management Journal, 22*(1), 13-22. Retrieved from http://www.asem.org/asemweb-emj.html

Auer-Rizzi, W., & Reber, G. (2013). Leadership styles: Inertia and changes in the Czech Republic. *Journal for East European Management Studies, 18*, 9-35. Retrieved from http://www.hampp-verlag.de/hampp_e-journals_JEMS.htm

Ayd, O. T. (2012). The impact of motivation and hygiene factors on research performance: An empirical study from a Turkish university. *International Review of Management and Marketing, 2*, 106-111. Retrieved from http://www.econjournals.com/index.php/irmm

Aydogdu, S., & Asikgil, B. (2011). The effect of transformational leadership behavior on organizational culture: An application in pharmaceutical industry. *International Review of Management and Marketing, 1*, 65-73. Retrieved from http://www.econjournals.com/index.php/irmm

Avey, J. B., Reichard, R. J., Luthans, F., & Mhatre, K. H. (2011). Meta-analysis of the impact of positive psychological capital on employee attitudes, behaviors, and performance. *Human Resource Development Quarterly, 22*, 127-152. doi:10.1002/hrdq.20070

Babcock-Roberson, M., & Strickland, O. J. (2010). The relationship between charismatic leadership, work engagement, and organizational citizenship behaviors. *The Journal of Psychology, 144*, 313-326. doi:10.1080/00223981003648336

Badshah, S. (2012). Historical study of leadership theories. *Journal of Strategic Human Resource Management, 1*(1), 49-59. Retrieved from http://www.manuscript.publishingindia.com/index.php/JSHRM

Bahreinian, M., Ahi, M., & Soltani, F. (2012). The relationship between personality type and leadership style of managers: A case study. *Mustang Journal of Business and Ethics, 3*, 94-111. Retrieved from http://www.mustangjournals.com/MJBE/MJBE_home.htm

Baser, I. U., & Rofcanin, Y. (2011). A scale development study on implicit leadership theories of selected management and MBA students from Turkey. *The Business Review, Cambridge, 17*(1), 129-133. Retrieved from http://www.jaabc.com/brc.html

Bass, B. M. (2008). *The Bass handbook of leadership: Theory, research, & managerial applications* (4th ed.). New York, NY: Free Press.

Bambale, A. J., Shamsudin, F. M., & Subramaniam, C. A. (2011). Stimulating organizational citizenship behavior (ocb) research for theory development: Exploration of leadership paradigms. *International Journal of Academic Research in Business and Social Sciences, 1*, 48-69. Retrieved from http://hrmars.com/index.php/pages/detail/IJARBSS

Baumgarten, M., Süß, H., & Weis, S. (2015). The cue is the key: The relevance of cues and contextual information in the social understanding tasks of the Magdeburg Test of Social Intelligence. *European Journal Of Psychological Assessment, 31*(1), 38-44. doi:10.1027/1015-5759/a000204

Bell, R. L., & Martin, J. S. (2012). The relevance of scientific management and equity theory in everyday managerial communication situations. *Journal of Management Policy and Practice, 13*(3), 106-115. Retrieved from http://www.na-businesspress.com/jmppopen.html

Benoliel, P., & Somech, A. (2014). The health and performance effects of participative leadership: Exploring the moderating role of the Big Five personality dimensions. *European Journal Of Work & Organizational Psychology, 23*, 277-294. doi:10.1080/1359432X.2012.717689

Bergman, J. Z., Rentsch, J. R., Small, E. E., Davenport, S. W., & Bergman, S. M. (2012). The Shared Leadership Process in Decision-Making Teams. *Journal Of Social Psychology, 152*, 17-42. doi:10.1080/00224545.2010.538763

Bildstein, I., Gueldenberg, S., & Tjitra, H. (2013). Effective leadership of knowledge workers: Results of an intercultural business study. *Management Research Review, 36*(8), 788-804. doi:http://dx.doi.org/10.1108/MRR-11-2012-0237

Boone, L. W., & Makhani, S. (2012). Five necessary attitudes of a servant leader. *Review of Business, 33*(1), 83-96. Retrieved from http://www.stjohns.edu/academics/schools-and-colleges/peter-j-tobin-college-business/journals

Boykins, C., Campbell, S., Moore, M., & Nayyar, S. (2013). An Empirical Study of Leadership Styles. *Journal Of Economic Development, Management, IT, Finance & Marketing, 5*(2), 1-31. Retrieved from http://www.gsmi-ijgb.com/Pages/JEDMITFM.aspx

Burian, P. E., Burian, P. S., Maffei III, F. R., & Pieffer, M. A. (2014). Principles driven leadership: Thoughts, observations and conceptual model. *International Journal of Management & Information Systems (Online), 18*, 1-10. Retrieved from http://www.cluteinstitute.com/journals/international-journal-of-management-information-systems-ijmis/

Burke, W. (2011). On the legacy of theory Y. *Journal of Management History, 17*, 193-201. doi:10.1108/17511341111112596

Cho, V., & Huang, X. (2012). Professional commitment, organizational commitment, and the intention to leave for professional advancement. *Information Technology & People, 25*(1), 31-54. doi:http://dx.doi.org/10.1108/09593841211204335

Choong, Y., Wong, K., & Lau, T. (2012). Organizational commitment: An empirical investigation on the academician of Malaysian private universities. *Business and Economics Research Journal, 3*(2), 51-64. Retrieved from http://www.berjournal.com/

Clark, C. R., Mercer, S. H., Zeigler-Hill, V., & Dufrene, B. A. (2012). Barriers to the success of ethnic minority students in school psychology graduate programs. *School Psychology Review, 41*, 176-192. Retrieved from http://www.nasponline.org/publications/spr/index-list.aspx

Choudhary, A. I., Akhtar, S. A., & Zaheer, A. (2013). Impact of transformational and servant leadership on organizational performance: A comparative analysis. *Journal of Business Ethics, 116*, 433-440. doi:10.1007/s10551-012-1470-8

Cockshaw, W., Shochet, I., & Obst, P. (2014). Depression and belongingness in general and workplace contexts: A cross-lagged longitudinal investigation. *Journal Of Social And Clinical Psychology, 33*, 448-462. doi:10.1521/jscp.2014.33.5.448

Cohen, A., Ben-Tura, E., & Vashdi, D. R. (2012). The relationship between social exchange variables, OCB, and performance. *Personnel Review, 41*, 705-731. doi:10.1108/00483481211263638

Colón, M., & Smith, S. H. (2012). Challenges to leadership in a transitioning environment. *Reflections, 18*(2), 77-81. Retrieved from http://www.reflectionsnarrativesofprofessionalhelping.org/index.php/Reflections/index

Darvish, H., & Rezaei, F. (2011). The impact of authentic leadership on job satisfaction and team commitment. *Management & Marketing, 6*, 421-436. Retrieved from http://www.managementmarketing.ro/

de Vries, R. E., Pathak, R. D., & Paquin, A. R. (2011). The paradox of power sharing: Participative charismatic leaders have subordinates with more instead of less need for leadership.

European Journal Of Work & Organizational Psychology, 20, 779-804. doi:10.1080/1359432X.2010.509923

Derue, D. S., Nahrgang, J. D., Wellman, N., & Humphrey, S. E. (2011). Trait and behavioral theories of leadership: An integration and meta-analytic test of their relative validity. *Personnel Psychology, 64*, 7-52. doi:10.1111/j.1744-6570.2010.01201.x

Dhiman, S. (2011). Personal mastery and authentic leadership. *Organization Development Journal, 29*(2), 69-83. Retrieved from http://www.isodc.org/

Drescher, M. A., Korsgaard, M. A., Welpe, I. M., Picot, A., & Wigand, R. T. (2014). The Dynamics of Shared Leadership: Building Trust and Enhancing Performance. *Journal of Applied Psychology, 99,* 771-83. doi:10.1037/a0036474

DuBois, M., Koch, J., Hanlon, J., Nyatuga, B., & Kerr, N. (2015). Leadership styles of effective project managers: Techniques and traits to lead high performance teams. *Journal Of Economic Development, Management, IT, Finance & Marketing 7*, no. 1: 30-46. Retrieved from http://www.gsmi-ijgb.com/Pages/JEDMITFM.aspx

Epitropaki, O. (2013). A multi-level investigation of psychological contract breach and organizational identification through the lens of perceived organizational membership: Testing a moderated-mediated model. *Journal Of Organizational Behavior, 34*, 65-86. doi:10.1002/job.1793

Erkutlu, H., & Chafra, J. (2013). Effects of trust and psychological contract violation on authentic leadership and organizational deviance. *Management Research Review, 36*, 828-848. doi:10.1108/MRR-06-2012-0136

Farr, J. & Brazil, D. (2009). Leadership skills development for engineers. *Engineering Management Journal, 21*(1), 3-8. Retrieved from http://www.asem.org/asemweb-emj.html

France, D., Leahy, M., & Parsons, M. (2009). Attracting, developing and retaining talent. *Research Technology Management, 52*(6), 33-44. Retrieved from http://www.iriweb.org:8080/Main/Library/RTM_Journal/Public_Site/Navigation/Publications/Research-Technology_Management/index.aspx?hkey=a684bca1-0bed-4520-83eb-b8e4df9c6b9b

Fulk, H., Bell, R. L., & Bodie, N. (2011). Team Management by Objectives: Enhancing Developing Teams' Performance. *Journal Of Management Policy & Practice, 12*(3), 17-26. Retrieved from aripd.org/jmpp

Galvin, T., Gibbs, M., Sullivan, J., & Williams, C. (2014). Leadership Competencies of Project Managers: An Empirical Study of Emotional, Intellectual, and Managerial Dimensions. *Journal Of Economic Development, Management, IT, Finance & Marketing, 6*(1), 35-60. Retrieved from http://www.gsmi-ijgb.com/Pages/JEDMITFM.aspx

Gardiner, R. A. (2011). A critique of the discourse of authentic leadership. *International Journal of Business and Social Science, 2*(15), 99-104. Retrieved from www.ijbssnet.com

Goh, S., & Zhen-Jie, L. (2014). The influence of servant leadership towards organizational commitment: The mediating role of trust in leaders. *International Journal of Business and Management, 9*(1), 17-25. doi:10.5539/ijbm.v9n1p17

Goleman, D., Boyatzis, R., & McKee, A. (2002). *Primal leadership: Realizing the power of emotional intelligence.* Boston. MA: Harvard Business School Press.

Hansen, S. D., Alge, B. J., Brown, M. E., Jackson, C. L., & Dunford, B. B. (2013). Ethical leadership: Assessing the value of a multifoci social exchange perspective. *Journal of Business Ethics, 115*, 435-449. doi:10.1007/s10551-012-1408-1

Harwiki, W. (2013). The influence of servant leadership on organization culture, organizational commitment, organizational citizenship behavior and employees' performance (study of outstanding cooperatives in East Java province, Indonesia). *Journal of Economics and Behavioral*

Studies, 5, 876-885. Retrieved from
http://www.ifrnd.org/JournalDetail.aspx?JournalID=2

Hu, J. & Liden, R. C. (2011). Antecedents of team potency and team effectiveness. An examination of goal and process clarity and servant leadership. *Journal of Applied Psychology, 96*, 851-862. doi:10.1037/a0022465

Huang, C. (2013). Shared leadership and team learning: Roles of knowledge sharing and team characteristics. *Journal of International Management Studies, 8*(1), 124-133. Retrieved from http://www.jimsjournal.org/

Ika, L. A., Diallo, A., & Thuillier, D. (2010). Project management in the international development industry. *International Journal of Managing Projects in Business, 3*, 61-93. doi:10.1108/17538371011014035

Kaminsky, J. B. (2012). Impact of nontechnical leadership practices on IT project success. *Journal Of Leadership Studies, 6*(1), 30-49. doi:10.1002/jls.21226

Karanja, E., & Zaveri, J. (2012). IT leaders: Who are they and where do they come from? *Journal of Information Systems Education, 23*, 143-163. Retrieved from http://jise.org/

Khaleefah, Q. Q., Rashid, F. A., Al Ajoe, A. Y., & AL-Husien, M. (2014). The foundations of project success work for small and medium businesses enterprises. *International Journal of Academic Research in Business and Social Sciences, 4*(12), 127-137. doi: 10.6007/IJARBSS/v4-i12/1333

Killian, K. D. (2012). Development and validation of the emotional self-awareness questionnaire: A measure of emotional intelligence. *Journal of Marital and Family Therapy, 38*, 502-14. doi:10.1111/j.1752-0606.2011.00233.x

Lian, L. K., & Tui, L. G. (2012). Leadership styles and organizational citizenship behavior: The mediating effect of subordinates' competence and downward influence tactics. *The Journal of Applied Business and Economics, 13*, 59-96. Retrieved from http://www.aebrjournal.org

Liaw, Y.-J., Chi, N.-W., & Chuang, A. (2010). Examining the mechanisms linking transformational leadership, employee customer orientation, and service performance: The mediating roles of perceived supervisor and coworker support. *Journal of Business and Psychology, 25*, 477-492. doi:10.1007/s10869-009-9145-x

Malangwasira, T. E. (2013). Demographic differences between a leader and followers tend to inhibit leader-follower exchange levels and job satisfaction. *Journal of Organizational Culture, Communication and Conflict, 17*(2), 63-106. Retrieved from http://www.alliedacademies.org/public/journals/JournalD etails.aspx?jid=11

McDermott, A. M., Conway, E., Rousseau, D. M., & Flood, P. C. (2013). Promoting effective psychological contracts through leadership: The missing link between HR strategy and performance. *Human Resource Management, 52*), 289-310. doi:10.1002/hrm.21529

Mishra, P., Dangayach, G. S., & Mittal, M. L. (2011). An empirical study on identification of critical success factors in project based organizations. *Global Business and Management Research, 3*(3), 356-368. Retrieved from http://www.gbmr.ioksp.com/

Morand, D. A., & Merriman, K. K. (2012). "Equality theory" as a counterbalance to equity theory in human resource management. *Journal of Business Ethics, 111*, 133-144. doi:10.1007/s10551-012-1435-y

Mukherjee, A. N. (2012). Steve Jobs to Narayana Murthy: Readdressing the conceptual metaphor of leadership. *International Journal of Management Research and Reviews, 2*, 354-376. Retrieved from http://ijmrr.com/

Muna, F. A. (2011). Contextual leadership. *The Journal of Management Development, 30*, 865-881. doi:10.1108/02621711111164349

Murray, A. (2011). Mind the gap: Technology, millennial leadership and the cross-generational workforce. *Australian Library Journal, 60*, 54-65. doi:10.1080/00049670.2011.10722556

Mutlucan, N. C. (2011). A conceptual model of the authentic leader's positive psychological capacities in the context of financial crisis. *The Business Review, Cambridge, 18*(1), 99-109. Retrieved from http://www.jaabc.com/brc.html

Nichols, T. W., & Erakovich, R. (2013). Authentic leadership and implicit theory: A normative form of leadership? *Leadership & Organization Development Journal, 34*, 182-195. doi:10.1108/01437731311321931

Nixon, P., Harrington, M., & Parker, D. (2012). Leadership performance is significant to project success or failure: A critical analysis. *International Journal of Productivity and Performance Management, 61*, 204-216. doi:10.1108/17410401211194699

Notgrass, D., Conner, C., & Bell, T. J. (2013). Leading external auditing teams: The correlation between leaders' behaviors and team dynamics of cohesion and conflict. *International Journal Of Business & Public Administration, 10*(2), 1-14. Retrieved from http://www.iabpad.com/IJBPA/

Nwokah, N. G., & Ahiauzu, A. I. (2010). Marketing in governance: Emotional intelligence leadership for effective corporate governance. *Corporate Governance, 10*, 150-162. doi:10.1108/14720701011035675

O'Boyle, E. H., Humphrey, R. H., Pollack, J. M., Hawver, T. H., & Story, P. A. (2011). The relation between emotional intelligence and job performance: A meta-analysis. *Journal of Organizational Behavior, 32*, 788-818. doi:10.1002/job.714

Ofori, D. F. (2013). Project management practices and critical success factors-A developing country perspective. *International Journal of Business and Management, 8*(21), 14-31. doi: 10.5539/ijbm.v8n21p14

Park, J., & Kwon, B. (2013). Literature Review on Shared Leadership in Teams. *Journal Of Leadership, Accountability & Ethics, 10*(3), 28-36. Retrieved from http://www.na-businesspress.com/jlaeopen.html

Parris, D. L., & Peachey, J. W. (2013). A systematic literature review of servant leadership theory in organizational contexts. *Journal of Business Ethics, 113*, 377-393. doi:10.1007/s10551-012-1322-6

Perez-Arostegui, M., Benitez-Amado, J., & Tamayo-Torres, J. (2012). Information technology-enabled quality performance: An exploratory study. *Industrial Management + Data Systems, 112*, 502-518. doi:10.1108/02635571211210095

Peus, C., Wesche, J. S., Streicher, B., Braun, S., & Frey, D. (2012). Authentic leadership: An empirical test of its antecedents, consequences, and mediating mechanisms. *Journal of Business Ethics, 107*, 331-348. doi:10.1007/s10551-011-1042-3

Powell, G. N., & Butterfield, D. A. (2011). Sex, gender, and the US presidency: Ready for a female president? *Gender in Management, 26*, 394-407. doi:10.1108/17542411111164894

Prindle, R. (2012). Purposeful resistance leadership theory. *International Journal of Business and Social Science, 3*(15), 9-13. Retrieved from http://www.ijbssnet.com

Rahim, M. A. (2014). A structural equations model of leaders' social intelligence and creative performance. *Creativity & Innovation Management, 23*(1), 44-56. doi:10.1111/caim.12045

Ramlall, S. (2012). A review of employee motivation theories and their implications for employee retention within organizations. *Journal of American Business Review, Cambridge., 1*(1), 189-200. Retrieved from http://www.jaabc.com/jabrc.html

Randmann, L. (2013). Managers on the both sides of the psychological contract. *Journal Of Management & Change, 30/31*(1/2), 124-144. Retrieved from http://www.ebs.ee/en/research-and-doctoral-studies/journal-of-management-and-change

Rivera-Ruiz, I., & Ferrer-Moreno, E. (2015). The relationship between strategic leadership, human IT infrastructure, project management, project success, and firm performance.

International Journal of Information, Business and Management,
7(2), 77-84. Retrieved from http://ijibm.elitehall.com/

Russ, T. L. (2011). Theory X/Y assumptions as predictors of
    managers' propensity for participative decision making.
    Management Decision, 49, 823-836.
    doi:10.1108/00251741111130887

Sahin, F. (2012). The mediating effect of leader-member exchange on
    the relationship between theory X and Y management styles
    and affective commitment: A multilevel analysis. *Journal of
    Management and Organization, 18,* 159-174.
    doi:10.5172/jmo.2012.18.2.159

Salter, C. R., Harris, M. H., Woodhull, M., & McCormack, J. (2013).
    A study of the relationship between moral maturity and
    respondent's self-rated leadership style. *Journal of Leadership,
    Accountability and Ethics, 10*(5), 96-108. Retrieved from
    http://www.na-businesspress.com/JLAE/jlaescholar.html

Sedgwick, M., Oosterbroek, T., & Ponomar, V. (2014). "It all
    depends": How minority nursing students experience
    belonging during clinical experiences. *Nursing Education
    Perspectives, 35*(2), 89-93. doi:10.5480/11-707.1

Skiba, M., & Rosenberg, S. (2011). The disutility of equity theory in
    contemporary management practice. *The Journal of Business
    and Economic Studies, 17*(2), 1-19, 97-98. Retrieved from
    http://management.njit.edu/jbes/index.php

Stagnaro, C., & Piotrowski, C. (2013). Shared leadership in IT project
    management: A practice survey. *International Journal of
    Management & Information Systems (Online), 17,* 223-233.
    Retrieved from
    http://www.cluteinstitute.com/journals/international-
    journal-of-management-information-systems-ijmis/

Thaliath, A., & Thomas, R. (2012). Motivation and its impact on
    work behavior of the employees of the IT industry in
    Bangalore. *Journal of Strategic Human Resource Management,
    1*(1), 60-67. Retrieved from

http://www.manuscript.publishingindia.com/index.php/JS HRM

Tudor, T. R. (2011). Motivating employees with limited pay incentives using equity theory and the fast food industry as a model. *International Journal of Business and Social Science, 2*(23), 95-101. Retrieved from http://www.ijbssnet.com

Turner, R., & Muller, R. (2005). The project manager's leadership style as a success factor on projects: A literature review. *Project Management Journal, 36*(2), 49-61. Retrieved from http://www.pmi.org/Learning/Publications-Project-Management-Journal.aspx

Wang, D., Waldman, D. A., & Zhang, Z. (2013). A Meta-Analysis of Shared Leadership and Team Effectiveness. *Journal Of Applied Psychology, 99*, 181-198. doi:10.1037/a0034531

Warner, J. (2012). Social capital and IS leadership: A conceptual framework. *Academy of Information and Management Sciences Journal, 15*, 85-98. Retrieved from http://www.alliedacademies.org/public/journals/journaldet ails.aspx?jid=10

Wikhamn, W., & Hall, A. T. (2012). Social exchange in a Swedish work environment. *International Journal of Business and Social Science, 3*(23), 56-64. Retrieved from http://www.ijbssnet.com

Xue, Y., Bradley, J., & Liang, H. (2011). Team climate, empowering leadership, and knowledge sharing. *Journal of Knowledge Management, 15*, 299-312. doi:http://dx.doi.org/10.1108/13673271111119709

Yan, J. (2011). An empirical examination of the interactive effects of goal orientation, participative leadership, and task conflict on innovation in small business. *Journal Of Developmental Entrepreneurship, 16*, 393-408. doi:10.1142/S1084946711001896

Yusof, H. M., Kadir, H. A., & Mahfar, M. (2014). The role of emotions in leadership. *Asian Social Science, 10*(10), 41-49. doi:10.5539/ass.v10n10p41

Zacher, H., & Jimmieson, N. L. (2013). Leader-follower interactions: Relations with OCB and sales productivity. *Journal of Managerial Psychology, 28*, 92-106. doi:10.1108/02683941311298887

Zacher, H., Pearce, L. K., Rooney, D., & Mckenna, B. (2014). Leaders' personal wisdom and leader-member exchange quality: The role of individualized consideration. *Journal of Business Ethics, 121*, 171-187. doi:10.1007/s10551-013-1692-4

Zehir, C., Akyuz, B., Eren, M. S., & Turhan, G. (2013). The indirect effects of servant leadership behavior on organizational citizenship behavior and job performance: Organizational justice as a mediator. *International Journal of Research in Business and Social Science, 2*(3), 1-13. Retrieved from http://www.ijbssnet.com

Recommended Reading List

Listed in no particular order by title and author(s):

1. Primal Leadership – Goleman, Boyatzis, McGee
2. The Leadership Challenge – Kouzes, Posner
3. How to Win Friends and Influence People (the original version) – Carnegie
4. What Got You Here Won't Get You There – Goldsmith
5. MOJO – Goldsmith
6. The Practical Drucker – Cohen
7. The World According to Peter Drucker – Beatty
8. The Effective Executive in Action – Drucker, Maciariello
9. Peter Drucker on the Profession of Management – Drucker
10. The Five Most Important Questions…- Peter Drucker, and others
11. On Becoming a Leader – Bennis
12. Judgment – Tichy, Bennis
13. The No A**hole Rule – Sutton

www.ingramcontent.com/pod-product-compliance
Lightning Source LLC
Chambersburg PA
CBHW070046210526
45170CB00012B/603

* 9 7 8 1 5 4 0 3 7 4 2 6 4 *